THE

MISSISSIPPI

BOOK OF

QUOTATIONS

BY DAVID CREWS

NAUTILUS PUBLISHING

The Mississippi Book of Quotations © copyright, 2022, David Crews

Disclaimer: *Many of the quotations in this book are attributed to fictional characters and are not necessarily the opinions of the author.*

ISBN: 978-1-949455-30-4

The Nautilus Publishing Company
426 South Lamar Blvd., Suite 16
Oxford, Mississippi 38655
Tel: 662-513-0159
www.nautiluspublishing.com

First Edition

Front cover design by Neil White.

Library of Congress Cataloging-in-Publication Data has been applied for.

Printed in Canada

10   9   8   7   6   5   4   3   2

To my soulful, courageous, literate, loving dad, John Crews

To my nurturing, devoted, tender mom, June Lowrey Crews

To the Boys of Spring and Lads of Sewanee

And especially to my wonderful, loving bride, son, and daughter —
Claire, Battle, and Caroline — who are the sweetest part of my life.

THE BOOK OF
MISSISSIPPI QUOTATIONS

THE BOOK OF
MISSISSIPPI QUOTATIONS

INTRODUCTION

Mississippi, a fiercely complex land, is both mesmerizing and baffling. Our country's most impoverished state is undeniably our richest when it comes to writing, lyrics, and stories. Economically poor, Mississippi is immeasurably rich in words and ideas that bubble to the surface in great literature, in songwriting, and in storytelling.

The Mississippi Book of Quotations brings together the artistry and cadences of the world's greatest storytellers. It blends powerful observations on love, truth, lies, race, women, war, humor, failure, fear, humility, evil, politics, religion, law, the blues, violence, drinking, death, endurance, and sacrifice — the wide breadth of themes and emotions that make up life well lived and poorly lived.

As those who dig deeply into this book will observe, cruelty and courage are close companions in a culture that spawned both Theodore Bilbo and Medgar Evers. Nobility and depravity exist side by side in this collection of quotations from novels, songs, essays, speeches, talk shows, conversation, and many other sources. Thankfully, the heartfelt, insightful, and uplifting far outweigh the dispiriting.

This volume includes quotations from accomplished writers, soulful musicians, sports heroes, civil rights icons, and everyday Mississippians. There are searing insights, homespun wisdom, banal absurdities, and raucous humor from over 250 observers including Eudora Welty, William Faulkner, Leontyne Price, Tennessee Williams, Fannie Lou Hamer, Oprah Winfrey, Elvis Presley, Archie Manning, Dizzy Dean, Muddy Waters, Shelby Foote, Donna Tartt, Beth Henley, Morgan Freeman, and John Grisham.

How it started

The idea for this book has been percolating for years. Starting in high school, I collected lines from Winston Churchill, Abraham Lincoln, the Bible, and other sources that I stumbled across while reading or in conversation with my dad, friends, and teachers, especially teachers like my fabulous high school English and Latin teacher, Oleatte Cearney, who in the tough, racially divisive 1960s courageously taught values, character, and understanding, as well as literature.

In time I realized that Mississippi writers were as rich and compelling as Shakespeare, Homer, Dickens, and Twain. I began to read Welty and Faulkner, whom I did not always understand, but persisted in trying to unravel. I persist to this day. Not only did I read Mississippi writers, but in our close-knit state, I was able to bump into Miss Eudora, Mr. Faulkner, Willie Morris, Larry Brown, and Shelby Foote, leading, on occasion, to unexpected encounters, not all of which involved drinking.

In the early 1980s, long before personal computers, the only place to get the *New York Times* was at Parkins Pharmacy next to the Jitney Jungle grocery in Jackson. On my way back to work following a lunchtime run, I would swing by Parkins to pick up the *Times* each day. On occasion, I would see Miss Eudora there also purchasing the *Times*. She would drive precariously through the streets of Belhaven to retrieve her paper. I immediately decided that if Miss Eudora wanted to read the *New York Times* each day that I would buy two and start delivering the paper to her doorstep.

The next day, I went to Parkins and purchased two papers. I pledged Bill behind the counter to secrecy. I then drove my truck to within a half block of Miss Welty's home, ran across her yard, deposited the *New York Times* on her doorstep, raced back to my truck, and drove to my office.

This ritual went on daily for about two weeks. One day, Bill took me aside and said, "Miss Welty was in here yesterday and asked if we were delivering her paper. I told her we were not delivering her paper." Miss Welty commented, "Well, it's the oddest thing; it appears on my doorstep each afternoon. Do you know who is bringing it?" Bill lied and assured her that he had no idea.

The next day, I arrived at Parkins, bought my two papers, drove to within a half block of her home, dashed across the yard, deposited the *New York Times*, and started running back across the yard.

At that moment, the door to Miss Welty's car flung open, and she rose up from a crouched position beneath the steering wheel and dramatically said, "Ah ha, I've found you out."

I introduced myself, and Miss Welty thanked me in that soft, special, genuine, grateful manner that was unique to her.

She then invited me into her home, whereupon we sat in her modest kitchen, and she served both of us a glass of Makers Mark whiskey. About once a month after that first encounter, Miss Welty would meet me at her door and invite me into her home for conversation and an early-afternoon whiskey. Miss Welty got her *New York Times* each day, but I've always felt I got the better end of the bargain.

Years earlier, I had a brief boyhood encounter with William Faulkner. When I was a youngster, my family left Mississippi for five years while my dad pursued his master's degree and Ph.D. at the University of Virginia. We lived on campus in drafty, poorly-built housing that had served as barracks for U.S. Marines during WWII.

Faulkner served as writer in residence at UVA for a brief but valuable stint. While in Charlottesville, Mr. Faulkner lived in a handsome antebellum mansion not far from my family's spartan quarters on Old Copely Hill. Like most young boys in those days, my brother Billy and I roamed far, wide, and mischievously throughout campus and town.

One day after playing for hours in the loft of a hay barn, we strolled past Faulkner's home. It was autumn, and there was a small apple orchard next to Faulkner's home. This orchard, full of apples, was irresistible to two young, semi-wayward, always-hungry lads. So I shimmied up one of the trees and started chunking apples down to my brother.

Unbeknownst to us, Mr. Faulkner walked out on his front porch, spied us, and walked down into the orchard. He looked up at me and said in a rather high-pitched voice for a man, "What are you boys doing?"

I was startled and immediately started stammering and searching for a convincing lie. I was not especially clever. After searching fruitlessly, all I could come up with was the truth and blurted out, "Well, sir, well, sir, we're stealing apples."

Perhaps disarmed by this unexpected bit of honesty, Mr. Faulkner chuckled under his breath and said, "Well, go right ahead."

Remarkably, the only time I ever met William Faulkner, I was stealing from him.

Now, it is possible that the man my brother and I encountered that day was not William Faulkner. I was very young and cared not a bit for literature beyond the Hardy Boys, *The Cat in the Hat*, and *Miss Minerva & William Green Hill*. My father had from a distance on campus one day pointed Faulkner out to me, telling me, "That is William Faulkner, a fine writer from our home state." So I had some inkling of what he looked like. The home where Faulkner lived at UVA is still there, and to this day it still has the small orchard enclosed by a low brick wall. As I've confessed, we stole apples that day and, admittedly, on other days.

All the signs agree that the man we encountered was William Faulkner. But even if it wasn't, who from Mississippi would tell the story any other way?

Who is included

Mississippians are friendly, generous, inclusive people, and this volume is generous, inclusive, and ecumenical when it comes to quotations. Most of those quoted are Mississippi natives. Several lived here for a substantial time or made a special mark while here. What writer or musician wouldn't want to be claimed and embraced by a state with so much rich material to offer? As the Arkansas poet Jo

McDougal commented, "If you want to be a writer, figure out a way to be born in Mississippi."

Several of those quoted here essentially have dual citizenship. Walker Percy was a product of Mississippi and Louisiana. The songwriter Rivers Rutherford was born right across the border in Memphis but attended college in Mississippi where he wrote his first song, "American Remains," recorded by The Highwaymen. While Peyton Manning may have been born down the road in New Orleans, he has deep roots here, thanks to his daddy from Drew and his momma from Neshoba County. It's well known, and it may even be a duly-passed law, that everyone in the Archie Manning clan is a Mississippian.

Not only are Mississippians liberally quoted, but figures outside our state often make remarkable comments about Mississippi. These include Abraham Lincoln, Ulysses S. Grant, William Tecumseh Sherman, John F. Kennedy, Martin Luther King, Jr., Teddy Roosevelt, Johnny Carson, and the cast of *Saturday Night Live,* who are all featured in the pages that follow.

Inevitably, I've left out some meaningful, poignant, heartfelt quotations. The quest for fine, pithy, revealing Mississippi quotations could last a lifetime, and perhaps it should. But publishers have deadlines. If those of you who dive into this book will pass along quotes that I missed or ran out of room for between these two covers, they will be strongly considered for any subsequent volume. Lord knows Mississippians will never stop writing, singing, and storytelling. There will always be room for a future and expanded volume of *The Mississippi Book of Quotations.*

These quotes will warm you, enrage you, amuse you, and entice you. I suspect readers will cringe in revulsion and cackle with delight. I might be wrong, but I don't think so.

David Crews, *August 6, 2016, Oxford, Mississippi*

ATTITUDE

Enthusiasm is the most important thing in life.
Tennessee Williams

The more you praise and celebrate your life, the
more there is in life to celebrate.
Oprah Winfrey

We are measured not by our victories and our losses,
but how we react to both.
Robert Khayat, *The Education of a Lifetime*

He never heard me say I would do anything but when
the time came to do it I didn't do it.
Holt Collier

If you can do it, it ain't braggin'.
Dizzy Dean

Sometimes you gotta mess up a little bit to wake up.
Archie Manning

When you start a mission, you have to finish a mission.
Jack Butler, *Jujitsu for Christ*

If the goddamn law won't take up for me, I'll take up for myself.
Larry Brown, *Father and Son*

The death threats made me angry. And I planned to use
that anger as fuel to fight this battle.
Robert Khayat, *The Education of a Lifetime*

I go crazy trying to energize people, 'cause that's what I am. I'm a
battery. If you're down, you can plug into me and get charged up.
Eli Manning

Luck is believing you're lucky.
Tennessee Williams

I became inured to defeat: I have never since expected victory.
William Alexander Percy

The main thing is the main thing.
Jim Barksdale

He was a lot bigger on the outside than on the inside.
Jack Butler, *Jujitsu for Christ*

Pressure is something you feel when you don't
know what the hell you're doing.
Peyton Manning

Be thankful for what you have; you'll end up having more. If you
concentrate on what you don't have, you will never, ever have enough.
Oprah Winfrey

The greatest discovery of all time is that a person can change
his future by merely changing his attitude.
Oprah Winfrey

This very moment is the only one you have for sure.
Oprah Winfrey

Turn your wounds into wisdom.
Oprah Winfrey

Unless you choose to do great things with it, it makes no difference how
much you are rewarded, or how much power you have.
Oprah Winfrey

You can have it all. You just can't have it all at once.
Oprah Winfrey

Doing the best at this moment puts you in the
best place for the next moment.
Oprah Winfrey

Luck is preparation meeting opportunity.
Oprah Winfrey

Passion is energy.
Oprah Winfrey

I don't think you ever stop giving. I think it's an ongoing process. And
it's not just about being able to write a check. It's being
able to touch somebody's life.
Oprah Winfrey

I don't give a shit.
David Crosby of the Byrds in response to Ole Miss student Flip Phillips asking if
his unknown band could open for the Byrds at Ole Miss. Phillips took this comment as
a yes and his band did, in fact, open for the Byrds.

I go through life with a smile because I know
things can be worse than they are.
Eli Manning

I don't think in the past. I don't think in the
future. You grasp the moment.
Eli Manning

I learned discipline, personal responsibility, the importance
of a strong spiritual life, and generosity.
Robert Khayat, *The Education of a Lifetime*

Now that's what I call hustle.
Barry Hannah, *The Tennis Handsome*

Mitch smiled and frowned at the same time.
John Grisham, *The Firm*

For more than twenty years, I defined my role of
CEO as Chief Encouraging Officer.
Charles Overby

Always be as kind to the janitor as you are to the CEO.
Judge Sharion Aycock

When a disaster strikes (Mississippi), before you can crawl out of the
rubble, a church van will pull up full of people
with chainsaws and casseroles.
Marshall Ramsey, *Chainsaws & Casseroles*

Persistence is the secret ingredient of life.
Marshall Ramsey, *Chainsaws & Casseroles*

If the Navy comes, they will build it.
Navy Secretary Ray Mabus

If you want to wear the uniform of this country and share in the honor
of its defense, then it does not matter what the color of your skin is,
your gender, or who you love. The only things that matter are
the ability to do the job and the willingness.
Navy Secretary Ray Mabus

Now let's cloud up and rain all over 'em.
Babe McCarthy, legendary MSU basketball coach

Boy, I gotta tell you, you gotta come out at 'em like a bitin' sow.
Babe McCarthy to his players

Cunning is better than strong.
Earnestine Moore

BASEBALL

I didn't know what to do. I'd never been that far before.
Harry Bush, when picked off third base

James "Cool Papa" Bell was so fast he could get out of bed, turn out
the lights across the room, and be back in bed under the
covers before the lights went out.
Josh Gibson, on Cool Papa Bell

Let me tell you about Cool Papa Bell. One time he hit a line drive right
past my ear. I turned around and saw the ball hit
his ass sliding into second.
Satchel Paige, on Cool Papa Bell

Yessuh, baseball is more than a little like life.
Red Barber

Doctor: Dizzy, your toe is fractured.
Dizzy Dean: Fractured, hell! The damn thing's broke.

I ain't what I used to be, but who the hell is?
Dizzy Dean

The good Lord was good to me. He gave me a strong body,
a good right arm, and a weak mind.
Dizzy Dean

I may not have been the greatest pitcher ever, but I was amongst 'em.
Dizzy Dean

X-RAYS OF DEAN'S HEAD SHOW NOTHING
Newspaper headline after Dean was knocked
in the head in the 1934 World Series

When Ole Diz was out there pitching, it was more than just another
ball game. It was a regular three-ring circus, and everybody
was wide awake and enjoying being alive.
Dizzy Dean

If Satch (Satchel Paige) and I were pitching on the same team, we'd cinch the pennant by July 4th and go fishing until World Series time.

Dizzy Dean

Today was the day of all days. Beat the mighty New York Yankees 5-0.

Boo Ferriss about his win in his second major
league game as a Boston Red Sox pitcher

Nobody in the history of baseball got off to a better
start than did Boo Ferriss in 1945.

Rick Cleveland, *Boo: A Life in Baseball*

He's for real. He can pitch.

Ted Williams, on Boo Ferriss

I learned the best way to pitch to Stan
"The Man" Musial. I walked him.

Boo Ferriss

BEAUTY

Beauty is terror. Whatever we call beautiful, we quiver before it.
Donna Tartt, *The Secret History*

What are artists? Desperate searchers after whatever
can be found of truth and beauty.
Tennessee Williams

Beauty is not a means, not a way of furthering a thing in the world. It is
a result; it belongs to ordering, to form, to aftereffect.
Eudora Welty

There is nothing wrong with the love of Beauty. But Beauty — unless
she is wed to something more meaningful — is always superficial.
Donna Tartt, *The Secret History*

…too beautiful to believe.
Donna Tartt, *The Secret History*

Beauty alters the grain of reality.
Donna Tartt, *The Goldfinch*

Isn't the point of things — beautiful things — that they connect you to
some larger beauty? Those first images that crack our heart wide open
and you spend the rest of our life chasing, or trying to
recapture, in one way or another?
Donna Tartt, *The Goldfinch*

The beauty of the present belongs to the fairies and children and
animals. The beauty of the future is held out to young men and
women. The beauty of the past is saved for old men.
Walter Anderson

A companionless soul could comfort itself with
the beauty of a well chosen word.
Kevin Sessums, *Mississippi Sissy*

BLUES

I've said that playing the blues is like having to be black twice.
B.B. King

Blues songs dwelt on hard work, violence, poverty, despair, wanderlust,
loneliness, drunkenness, and incarceration, which were
so much a part of black life in the Delta.
James Cobb, *The Most Southern Place on Earth*

The blues are the true facts of life expressed in words and
song, inspiration, feeling, and understanding.
Willie Dixon

The Mississippi sound, that Delta sound is in them
old records. You can hear it all the way through.
Muddy Waters

I was raised on blues and spirituals, but after you wake up to a lot of
facts about life, the spiritual thing starts to look kind of phony in places.
Willie Dixon

Jazz is the big brother of the blues.
B.B. King

The blues was like that problem child you may have had in the family.
You was a little bit ashamed to let anybody see him, but you loved him.
You just didn't know how other people would take it.
B.B. King

Be a Baptist preacher, and I sure won't have to work.
Son House, "Preachin' the Blues"

He had been shot, stabbed, pinned under a fallen tree, crushed under a
car he was working on when the jack slipped. He had twenty-six
children that he knew about, but he doubted that was all of them.
Richard Grant, *Dispatches from Pluto*, on blues singer T-Model Ford

I had a happy home,
And I wouldn't stay there.
Mattie Delaney, "Down the Big Road Blues"

The blues is a lowdown shakin' chill.
Robert Johnson, "Preachin' Blues"

I am the blues
The whole world knows
I've been mistreated and misused.
Willie Dixon, "I Am the Blues"

I been in the blues all my life. I'm still delivering
'cause I got a long memory.
Muddy Waters

I stone got crazy when I saw somebody run down them strings with a
bottleneck. My eyes lit up like a Christmas tree,
and I said that I had to learn.
Muddy Waters

I got up one Christmas morning, and we didn't have nothing to eat. We
didn't have an apple; we didn't have an orange; we didn't
have a cake; we didn't have nothing.
Muddy Waters

People should hear the pure blues — the blues we
used to have when we had no money.
Muddy Waters

Saturday night is your big night. Everybody used to fry up fish and have
one hell of a time. Find me playing 'til sunrise for fifty
cents and a sandwich. And be glad of it.
Muddy Waters

I call myself a blues singer, but you ain't never heard
me call myself a blues guitar man.
B.B. King

If you want to be a good blues singer, people are going to be down on you, so dress like you're going to the bank to borrow money.

B.B. King

The blues is good for me when I'm feeling bad
and good for me when I'm feeling good.

B.B. King

…The blues. It was not an ancient ancestral moan but the cry of alienated, uprooted modern man, craving independence and strongly individualistic in a way that African music had never been.

Richard Grant, *Dispatches from Pluto*

CHARACTER

When we come to a crossroads, character must take over.
Sam Haskell, *Promises I Made My Mother*

…by a simple act of decency, he had placed himself beyond the pale of his own tribe and put his job, his life, and his family at risk.
Greg Iles, *Natchez Burning*

They are victims of that whole generation of their fathers, teachers, governors, who promulgate and put on public record the postulate of national fear of our national character: that Americans as individuals or in the mass are incapable of independence, courage, endurance, sacrifice; that in time of trouble and crisis, we will not hold together since our character is not in the brain nor the heart, but in the appetites, the entrails.
William Faulkner, on cadets dismissed from U.S. Military Academy

The character, I don't forget, and when the book is finished, that character is not done, he is still going on at some new devilment that sooner or later I will find out about and write about.
William Faulkner to UVA class

Some mystery should be left in the revelation of character in a play, just as a great deal of mystery is always left in the revelation of character in life, even in one's own character to himself.
Tennessee Williams

There's nothing harder than fighting alone, with no one to keep you company in your foxhole.
Greg Iles, *The Bone Tree*

I suppose there is a certain crucial interval in everyone's life when character is fixed forever.
Donna Tartt, *The Secret History*

CHILDREN

A barn is a wondrous place to children.
Tom Franklin, *Crooked Letter, Crooked Letter*

This may be good for the children… It will be teaching them at an early and tender age to be ever on guard to protect and shield their elders and teachers from certain of the simple facts of life.
William Faulkner, on the deletion of "hell" from a high school text of *Two Soldiers*

I'm a firm believer that the first two tenets of effective child-rearing boil down to spend a lot of time with your children and cherish them, because, one, they need you when they're growing, and, two, they're going to be up and gone before you realize it.
Archie Manning

He was a teenager. He was not patient.
Jack Butler, *Jujitsu for Christ*

When grown people speak of the innocence of children, they don't really know what they mean. There is no crime which a boy of eleven has not envisaged long ago. His only innocence is he may not yet be old enough to desire the fruits of it, which is not innocence but appetite; his innocence is, he does not know how to commit it, which is not ignorance, but size.
William Faulkner, *The Reivers*

All you have to do to educate a child is leave him alone and teach him to read. The rest is brainwashing.
Ellen Gilchrist, *Falling Through Space*

I love to watch them (children) work on their mothers to get what they want, and, because I am always a child, I'm pulling for them to get the candy and to get it NOW. The other day, I watched a little blond beauty pull her mother's face to her and lay her hands on her mother's cheeks and kiss her nose. Needless to say, they opened the bag of cookies then and there.
Ellen Gilchrist, *The Writing Life*

The Faulkners are anticipating a blessed expense.

Walter Winchell, on the imminent birth of Jill Faulkner

There are too many Faulkner boys anyway.

William Faulkner, on the birth of his daughter, Jill

Little children, as long as they are little children, shall be
intact, unanguished, untorn, unterrified.

William Faulkner

Getting close to books, and spending time by myself, I was obliged to
think about things I would never have thought about if I
was busy romping around with a brother and sister.

Shelby Foote

Children love secret club houses. They love secrecy even
when there's no need for secrecy.

Donna Tartt

Children — if you think back really what it was like to be a child and
what it was like to know other children — children lie all the time.

Donna Tartt

The books I loved in childhood — the first loves — I've read so often
that I've internalized them in some really essential way;
they are more inside me now than out.

Donna Tartt

It is a terrible thing to learn as a child that one is a being separate from
all the world, that no one and no thing hurts along with one's burned
tongues and skinned knees, that one's aches and pains are all one's own.

Donna Tartt, *The Secret History*

The faith of children is an awesome thing to behold.
If only we could all be worthy of it.

Greg Iles, *Natchez Burning*

Lester was a doting father until the little girl began to
talk, and he realized she had nothing to say.

Bill Dunlap, *Short Mean Fiction*

You either live in the same town with your children,
or you don't. There is no in-between.
Neil White, *In the Sanctuary of Outcasts*

A large abiding mimosa tree presided over the front yard of my
childhood home, and it made a perfect primer for tree climbing...
A mimosa grows in the shape of a beckon.
Jim Dees, *Lies and Other Truths*

Keep 'em in school, teach 'em to read, and get 'em to church.
Reverend Robert Jamison, on child rearing

My decision to become a lawyer was irrevocably sealed when I realized
my father hated the legal profession.
John Grisham

CIVIL RIGHTS

I'm sick and tired of being sick and tired.
Fannie Lou Hamer

You can kill a man, but you can't kill an idea.
Medgar Evers

Times of crisis are times for greatness.
Reverend Duncan Gray in 1954, on the civil rights movement

A map of Mississippi was a reminder not of geography, but of atrocities.
Myrlie Evers

A person is no better off enjoying nine of ten rights than they are none of ten. My thing is the whole hog; either all citizenship rights or none.
James Meredith

I don't know nothing about Communism. I know about Hungryism.
Fannie Lou Hamer

If I fall, I fall five feet and one quarter inches
forward in the fight for freedom.
Fannie Lou Hamer

So many people say that I was born too soon, but
that's not true. They opened the doors too late.
James Thomas "Cool Papa" Bell, on not playing in the Majors

I'm just as proud of it as anybody who came over on the Mayflower.
Leontyne Price on her African-American heritage

Accomplishments have no color.
Leontyne Price

I considered myself an active-duty soldier. I was at war, and
everything I did I considered an act of war.
James Meredith, on his campaign to enter Ole Miss

I am making this move in what I consider the interest of and for the benefit of my country, my race, my family, and myself.

James Meredith, letter to Thurgood Marshall of the NAACP

The only way I know to keep him (Meredith) out is just don't let him in.

Ross Barnett

Which one of you is Meredith?

Ross Barnett to a group of U.S. Justice Department Officials surrounding Meredith, who was the only black man in the group

Governor, I am concerned about this situation down there.

President Kennedy to Ross Barnett

There can be only one resolution to this crisis: the admission of James Meredith to the university.

Sermon by **Rev. Duncan Gray, Jr.**

We're not playing.

Sergeant Buford Babb, Miss. National Guard holding off rioters with bayonet

No matter what happens, we are going through. I'm gonna order the mob to disperse. If they don't, we're gonna go through them. Fire above their heads. Fire down at their feet. If that doesn't work, the shotgun squad will fire point blank, 'cause we are going through them regardless of what happens.

Lieutenant Donnie Bowman, U.S. Army, to his troops marching into the riot on the Ole Miss campus

I just don't remember it as being that bad.

Governor Haley Barbour, on the White Citizens' Council

You heard of the Citizens' Councils. Up north, they think it was like the KKK. Where I come from, it was an organization of town leaders.

Governor Haley Barbour

The NAACP lives by the Holy Bible and the Constitution of the United States of America, and as long as those two noble documents are kept alive, the NAACP will continue to fight, here in Mississippi, for those things that they guarantee —
Life, Liberty, and the Pursuit of Happiness.

Medgar Evers

I'm very hygienic, I bathe every day, and
I assure you this brown won't rub off.
Medgar Evers in an interview with IHL Board regarding his 1954
application for admission to the Ole Miss Law School

Mississippi is home. It is a part of the United States. And whether the
whites like it or not, I don't plan to live here as a parasite.
The things that I don't like, I will try to change.
Medgar Evers in a 1958 interview in *Ebony*

To hell with getting beat up! If a white man touched my wife, I'd fight
back or die in the attempt. They'd have to kill me to stop me!
I'd be less than a man not to fight back.
Medgar Evers

How much better to have turbulence to effect improvement,
rather than turbulence to maintain a stand-pat policy.
Medgar Evers

Do not attempt to underestimate the forces of resistance, ignorance,
trickery, threats, and physical assaults that have been employed. But
their eradication will not be accomplished by some miracle out of the
sky, some wished-for relief from a far-off place; it will be done
primarily through the intelligence, diligence, persistence, and
courage of the population presently disenfranchised.
Medgar Evers

I'm from Mississippi, where the state flag incorporates the Confederate
symbol. Over time, I became accustomed to serving as a convenient
scapegoat for Mississippi's civil rights-era crimes. I once received a
reprimand from a German, to whom I responded that if my homeland
had been responsible for the Holocaust, I would most assuredly keep
my opinions about other people's human rights violations to myself.
Alan Huffman, *We're With Nobody*

Mississippi is a better state today because of James Meredith.
Morgan Freeeman

I'm proud of my enemies. They're every color
but white, every creed but Christian.
Byron de La Beckwith
I've put up with more humiliation than I care to remember.
B.B. King

When you grow up in a totally segregated society, where everybody
around you believes that segregation is proper, you have a hard time.
You can't believe how much it's a part of your thinking.
Shelby Foote

No school will be integrated in Mississippi while I am your governor.
Ross Barnett, 1962

Ross Barnett is an inflexible racist with a mind relatively innocent of
history, constitutional law, and the processes of government.
Dr. James Silver

Why squander money on Negro education when the only effect is to
spoil a good field hand and make an insolent cook?
James K. Vardaman

Segregation is a stain on our nation's soul.
Senator Trent Lott in a statement regarding his
controversial remarks on Strom Thurmond

Excellence is the best deterrent to racism or sexism.
Oprah Winfrey

There are those who are alive, yet will never live.
There are those who are dead, yet will live forever.
Great deeds inspire and encourage the living.
Inscription on James Chaney's tombstone

Things have come a long way in Mississippi. Perhaps nowhere else in
America has made more progress in its race relations, but
then again, nowhere else had so far to go.
Richard Grant, *Dispatches from Pluto*

Mississippi had the most lynchings, the worst Klan violence, the staunchest resistance to the civil rights movement.
Richard Grant, *Dispatches from Pluto*

This, nor any other country or community of people, can no more get along in peace with ten percent of its population arbitrarily unassimilated than a town of five thousand people can get along in peace with five hundred unbridled horses loose in the streets, or say a community of five thousand cats with five hundred unassimilated dogs among them, or vice versa.
William Faulkner, address to Raven, Jefferson, and ODK Societies

This nation cannot endure containing a minority as large as ten percent held second class in citizenship by the accident of physical appearance. For peaceful co-existence, all must be one thing — either all first class citizens, or all second class citizens.
William Faulkner

To live anywhere in the world today and be against equality because of race or color is like living in Alaska and being against snow.
William Faulkner, *On Fear*

Negros... who could worship the white man's God but not in the white man's church; pay taxes in the white man's courthouse, but couldn't vote in it or for it; working by the white man's clock, but having to take his pay by the white man's counting.
William Faulkner, *On Mississippi*

A lonely, taciturn, and quixotic man of courage and purpose.
Arthur Schlesinger, Jr., on James Meredith

The North could be as cruel as the South to blacks.
Greg Iles, *Natchez Burning*

Dick Molpus is a real person with a real record on civil rights. We could remain smugly satisfied that we just randomly slammed a dude because he had a funny name like Dick Molpus. We could have looked up his record. But we didn't because I'm a 12-year-old boy trapped in a 75 year-old's body.
Jon Stewart, *The Daily Show*

Dick Molpus has a long and distinguished record of speaking out for civil rights in Mississippi. He is an honorable and good man who, in the 1990s, led the charge on big voting rights reforms. In 1989, Molpus spoke at a 25th anniversary memorial for the three civil rights activists murdered outside Philadelphia, Mississippi, a speech that earned Mr. Molpus death threats.

Jon Stewart, *The Daily Show*

Three mothers' sons died here in Neshoba County on June 21, 1964... we are not talking about abstractions, but about human beings.

Dick Molpus

Neshoba County is the worst place I've ever been in my life.

Dr. Martin Luther King, Jr.

I want to talk about the living dead that we have right among our midst, not only here in the state of Mississippi, but throughout the nation. Those are the people who don't care. And those who do care, but don't have guts enough to stand up for it (freedom).

David Dennis, Director of CORE in Mississippi, giving the eulogy at James Chaney's funeral

I'm sick and tired of going to the funerals of black men who have been murdered by white men... I'm sick and tired, and I ask you to be sick and tired with me.

David Dennis, eulogy for James Chaney

I'd vote against Jesus Christ if he was nominated for that position.

Senator Jim Eastland, regarding the nomination of Burke Marshall as Assistant Attorney General for Civil Rights

All whites are created equal with certain rights, among these are life, liberty, and the pursuit of dead niggers.

Senator Jim Eastland, 1956 speech to the White Citizens' Council

The Constitution of the U.S. was destroyed because the Supreme Court disregarded the law and decided that integration was right. You are not required to obey any court which passes out such a ruling. In fact, you are obligated to defy it.

Senator Jim Eastland, on Brown v. Board

We in the South can bring this nation out to human decency and humane respect, but to do that, people must realize that whether he's white as a sheet or black as a skillet, out of one blood God made all people.
Fannie Lou Hamer

I guess this is another one of those nigra versus white folks cases.
Judge Harold Cox

If the Fifth Circuit saw Judge Harold Cox's name on an opinion from Mississippi, they would reverse it without hardly looking at it.
Anonymous attorney, on Judge Harold Cox's decisions on civil rights issues

I may be a bigot, but I'm not a racist.
Judge Harold Cox

Church members confront the issue of race time and time again outside the church, but there he can deal with it in terms of law, economics, and custom. But within the parish church, he must wrestle with it on the level of conscience, morality, and religion… He must have the opportunity to wrestle and to struggle with the real issue for the sake of his own soul.
Reverend Duncan Gray

Courage was growing in me. Little by little, it was getting harder and harder for me not to speak out.
Anne Moody, *Coming of Age in Mississippi*

The courage that (MSU President) Colvard and (Babe) McCarthy showed in defying the Mississippi Legislature and fiery segregationist Gov. Ross Barnett to enable the all-white MSU men's basketball team to compete against a Loyola team with four African-American starters represented the university's finest hour.
Sid Salter, *Jack Cristil: Voice of the MSU Bulldogs*

I don't see anything morally wrong playing against Negroes, Indians, Russians or any other race or nationality.
MSU basketball player Leland Mitchell, 1963, on playing Loyola University with four black players

I think that Mississippi State wants to play us.
If they don't, they'll never know how good they are.
Jerry Harkness, Loyola University basketball player, 1963

CIVIL WAR

When the sun of the Union sets, it will go down in blood.
LQC Lamar

Still powerful, still dangerous, still coming.
William Faulkner, on the image of Nathan Bedford Forrest 75 years after his death

It's all now you see. Yesterday won't be over until tomorrow, and
tomorrow began ten thousand years ago. For every Southern boy
fourteen years old, not once but whenever he wants it, there is the
instant when it's still not yet two o'clock on that July afternoon in 1863,
the brigades are in position… waiting for Longstreet to give the
word, and it's all in the balance; it hasn't happened
yet; it hasn't even begun yet.
William Faulkner, *Intruder in the Dust*

…not even a regiment yet, but merely a voluntary association of un-
tried men who knew they were ignorant and hoped they were brave.
William Faulkner, *Requiem for a Nun*

We fought them mounted; we fought them dismounted, standing, or
running, all over that blasted field… there was
never a let-up until the thing was done.
Shelby Foote, *Shiloh*

More rain, more rest.
Shelby Foote, *Shiloh*

Captain, give me a gun. This damned fight ain't got any rear.
Shelby Foote, *Shiloh*, wounded soldier upon returning to the battle front

War was more shovelry than chivalry.
Shelby Foote, *Shiloh*

He was obeying his instinct for never standing to receive an
attack when he had a chance to deliver one.
Shelby Foote, *Shiloh*, on Nathan Bedford Forrest

Lee is a very complex man, but he had achieved simplicity.
Shelby Foote, on Robert E. Lee

The Civil War... the last romantic and the first modern war combined.
Shelby Foote to William Thomas, *Commercial Appeal*

The Civil War was the crossroads of our
being, and it was a hell of a crossroads.
Shelby Foote

Shiloh is a wonderfully dramatic battle. The leader of one side is killed,
and the other one is going on to glory, and it was the first great battle.
Shelby Foote

I'm crazy about Grant: his character, his nature,
his science of fighting, and everything else.
Shelby Foote

I had about fifty fist fights in my life. Out of those fifty fist fights, the
ones that I had the most vivid memory of were the ones I lost. I think
that's one reason why the South remembers
the war more than the North does.
Shelby Foote

Forrest… was amenable to no known rules of procedure, was a law
unto himself for all military acts, and was constantly
doing the unexpected at all times and places.
Shelby Foote, *The Beleaguered City*

He wasn't worth the powder it would take to blow him up.
Shelby Foote

I saw troubles innumerable.
Jefferson Davis

I make no terms. I accept no compromise.
Jefferson Davis

…there is no glory like Jeb Stuart putting spurs in his
sorrel and escaping the Minie balls.
Barry Hannah, *Airships*, "Knowing He Was Not My Kind…"

The Civil War was not started by Harriet Beecher Stowe, as Lincoln said, or by Sir Walter Scott, as Mark Twain said, or by economics, as somebody said. It was started by a thousand towns like this, bored out of their minds.

Barry Hannah, *Hey, Jack!*

I will yield to my general, who led me through four years of bloody war, but never led me through any danger.

Congressman "Private" John Allen, taunting an ex-general and fellow congressman who remained behind the front lines during battle.

We killed each other as fast as we could.

Soldier's description of the Battle of Champion's Hill

It shall be done.

Message from **General William Tecumpseh Sherman** to General Ulysses S. Grant responding to difficult orders at Vicksburg

I would like to talk to you.

Message from **General Ulysses S. Grant** to General William Tecumpseh Sherman while Grant was in Oxford and Sherman was ten miles away at College Hill

-

The past is dead; let it bury its dead, its hopes, and its aspirations; before you lies the future. Let me beseech you to lay aside all rancor, all bitter sectional feelings, and to take your places in the ranks of those who will bring about a consummation devoutly to be wished for — a reunited country.

Jefferson Davis' last public speech

The atmosphere in Mississippi was 'dense with horrid narratives of his negligence, whoring, and drunkenness. An acquittal by a court-martial of angels would not relieve him of the charge.'

James Phelan in letter to Jefferson Davis castigating General Earl Van Dorn during court-martial proceedings

Mississippians don't know, and refuse to learn, how to surrender.

Colonel James Autry at Vicksburg

War is a species of passionate insanity.

Mary Ann Loughborough at Vicksburg

Had Stonewall Jackson died to create a nation of couch potatoes ignorant of their own history and incapable of simple mathematics? If those brave soldiers in blue and gray had seen what lay in the future, they would have laid down their muskets and walked home to their farms.

Greg Iles, *True Evil*

CULTURE

A hundred years from now, the archaeologists
will go digging around here and find nothing.
William Faulkner, on Hollywood

If we in America have reached that point in our desperate culture when
we must murder children, no matter for what reason or color, we don't
deserve to survive and probably won't.
William Faulkner, on the murder of Emmett Till

Which is a better world... this fornicating Happyland USA or a Roman
Legion under Marcus Aurelius? Which is worse, to die with T.J. Jackson
at Chancellorsville or live with Johnny Carson in Burbank?
Walker Percy

All truly civilized people — the ancients no less than us — have civilized themselves through the willful repression of the old, animal self.
Donna Tartt, *The Secret History*

One place understood helps us understand all places better.
Eudora Welty

DEATH

If you don't think about death, you don't appreciate life.
John Grisham, *The Firm*

Blanche: Funerals are pretty compared to deaths.
Tennessee Williams, *A Streetcar Named Desire*

Your father has to die, better he dies in your arms.
Richard Ford

No wonder she wants to die. If all I had to watch was a soap opera
or a rerun of *Dallas*, I'd be ready to die, too.
Larry Brown, *Dirty Work*

Certainly I would be less frightened of death… if I thought
a familiar person came to meet us at the door.
Donna Tartt, *The Goldfinch*

We won't forget you just because you've up and died. We
may even like you better and visit you more often.
Gayden Metcalfe, *Being Dead is No Excuse*

The worst death I can imagine is a long life on Death Row.
Slim Smith, *Columbus Dispatch* columnist

Tell me the truth about death. I don't know what it is. We have them;
they are gone but they stay in our minds. Their stories are part of us as
long as we live and as long as we tell them or write them down.
Ellen Gilchrist, *Good Housekeeping*

When I get where I'm going, there'll be only happy tears. I will shed the
sins and struggles I have carried all these years.
Rivers Rutherford, "When I Get Where I'm Going"

He died. That's not such a bad thing.
John Grisham, *The Summons*

They say everyone's gonna be dying someday. I believe it too.
Beth Henley, *Miss Firecracker*

Rusty McDeere. Age eighteen, forever. (Killed in Vietnam)
John Grisham, *The Firm*

An odd thing about New Orleans: the cemeteries here are more
cheerful than the hotels and the French Quarter. Tell me why…
two thousand dead Creoles should be more alive
than two thousand live Buick dealers?
Walker Percy, *Lancelot*

Yuh die ef yuh fight! Yuh die if yuh don' fight! Either way yuh die 'n' it
don't mean nothin'.
Richard Wright, *Long Black Song*

Death is one moment, and life is so many of them.
Tennessee Williams

Is Phoenix Jackson's grandson really dead?
Eudora Welty, the question most asked of Miss Welty

Even though he's dead, the instinct to be afraid for her son is still there.
Kathryn Stockett, *The Help*

It's a fine funeral when someone plays the banjo.
Greg Bullock, Prentiss County

If I must die for this cause, then I have already been dead
a long time, and of what value is life to a dead man?
James Meredith, September 30, 1962

Dueling… appeared to be a leading cause of death among Mississippi's
embattled newspaper editors, four of whom were
gunned down in Vicksburg alone.
David Oshinsky, *Worse than Slavery*, on dueling in the 1800s

An epidemic death rate without the epidemic.
Frank Johnston, on deaths from the convict-leasing system in Mississippi

Our ancestors have been dying for hundreds of years,
and we plan to continue this tradition.
Gayden Metcalfe, *Being Dead Is No Excuse*

I'd never see anybody if I didn't go to funerals.
Gayden Metcalfe, *Being Dead Is No Excuse*

Though I be dead, this soil that holds me fast will find me breath.
William Faulkner, "My Epitaph"

My father died in my arms. That's tumult. That's everything exploding.
Richard Ford

They worship death here. They don't worship
money; they worship death.
William Faulkner, on Hollywood

Everybody wants to go to Heaven, but no one wants to die to get there.
B.B. King

Don't look forward to the day you stop suffering,
because when it comes, you'll know you're dead.
Tennessee Williams

She died... without pain, as they say, and whatever they mean by that.
William Faulkner

...a little nearer now was the moment, instant, night: dark: sleep: when
I would put it all away forever that I anguished and sweated over, and it
would never trouble me anymore.
William Faulkner, letter to the American Academy for the Howells Medal

...not like sentinels, defending the living from the dead...
but rather, the dead from the living.
William Faulkner, *Sepulture South*

...all a man had was time, all that stood between him and
the death he feared and abhorred was time.
William Faulkner, *Intruder in the Dust*

It's not men who cope with death: they resist, try to
fight back and get their brains trampled out.
William Faulkner, *The Reivers*

…Nature (meaning Death) always wins, but that
doesn't mean we have to bow and grovel to it.
Donna Tartt, *The Goldfinch*

Because death is the end, and if a man doesn't speak before it silences
him, then the things he holds closest die with him.
Greg Iles, *The Death Factory*

God is merely a part of the human brain, an evolutionary coping
mechanism that developed to make bearable our
awareness of our own deaths.
Greg Iles, *The Footprints of God*

…at least with dying there's the comfort of
knowing it's unlikely to happen again.
Stuart Stevens, *The Last Season*

Seems like nothin' ever come to no good up on Choctaw Ridge
And now Billie Joe MacAllister jumped off the Tallahatchie Bridge.
Bobbie Gentry, "Ode to Billie Joe"

What a small hole to lose a life out of.
Aden Fisher White, on the bullet wound that killed her father

Their crime was barbaric. Death is too good for them, much too good.
John Grisham, *A Time to Kill*

THE DELTA

I've always been glad that I enjoyed dances and helling around the
Delta. It's where I got much of the material I use…
Shelby Foote

Pure soil, endlessly deep, dark and sweet, dripping fatness.
David Cohn, describing the Mississisppi Delta

The Delta… seemed strummed, as though it were an instrument…
Eudora Welty, *Delta Wedding*

The Mississippi Delta shines like a national guitar.
Paul Simon, "Graceland"

The Mississippi Delta begins in the lobby of the Peabody Hotel in
Memphis and ends on Catfish Row in Vicksburg.
David Cohn, *Where I Was Born and Raised*

Cremation… is a new and dicey proposition in the Delta. The last time
somebody was cremated, his ashes were sprinkled from a crop duster.
We all ran for cover. We liked him fine, but we didn't want
him all over our good clothes.
Gayden Metcalfe, *Being Dead Is No Excuse*

The Delta, relentless and abiding… where the people
played seven-card stud against God.
Willie Morris

We were running all over the front lawn and under the rainspouts, barefooted, in our underpants, with the rain pelting down,
straight, cold, gray rain of Delta summers.
Ellen Gilchrist, *Light Can Be Both Wave and Particle*

If you stand near its fountain in the middle of the lobby,
where ducks waddle… ultimately you will see
everybody who is anybody in the Delta.
David Cohn

Memphis is the capital of the Delta.
Shelby Foote, to Robert Richards

The Yazoo-Mississippi alluvial delta… was the exclusive domain of
moccasins, bears, alligators, and panthers.
Shelby Foote, *The Beleaguered City*

What we like about this land most of all is the
sense of togetherness it gives.
Hodding Carter, *Where Main Street Meets the River*

This is a church-going and whiskey-drinking society.
David Cohn, *Where I Was Born and Raised*

Mary Bruce came to stay for six weeks and remained for eight years.
David Cohn, *Where I was Born and Raised*, on Delta hospitality

…A land of huge plantations, feudalistic in many ways, cotton-
intoxicated, Negro-obsessed, fearing the wrath of
God and the Mississippi River.
David Cohn, *Where I Was Born and Raised*

A person from the hills would never understand the
Coast and never be accepted in the Delta.
John Grisham, *The Summons*

If out of the 1927 flood our people learned mutual helpfulness… and
our government learned the necessity for flood control, we Delta folks
will have to pronounce that flood an unqualified success… though I
hope even the liveliest appreciation would not require
me to want to go through it again.
William Alexander Percy, *Lanterns on the Levee*

…wildest girl in the Mississippi Delta.
Ellen Gilchrist, *Traveler*

The Mississippi Delta is the most Southern place on earth.
James Cobb

Thoughts went out of her head and landscape filled
it. In the Delta, most of the world seemed sky.
Eudora Welty, *Delta Wedding*

...sixty girls from all over the Delta come to giggle in one house.
Eudora Welty, *Delta Wedding*

The land was perfectly flat and level, but it shimmered
like the wing of a lighted dragonfly.
Eudora Welty, *Delta Wedding*

In 1900, the Negro population stood at 89% in the Delta. There were
more blacks in Bolivar County than in all of Massachusetts. The 377
blacks living in North Dakota would make a disappointing
turnout at the funeral of a Delta Negro preacher.
David Oshinsky, *Worse Than Slavery*

People in the Delta look better dead, whether
in their coffins or obituaries.
Gayden Meltalfe, *Being Dead Is No Excuse*

If you don't get at least one caramel cake when you die in
the Delta, somebody doesn't love you.
Gayden Metcalfe, *Being Dead Is No Excuse*

The Delta was the soul and the heart. Mother
blues. Sacred, fertile ground.
Ace Atkins, *Crossroad Blues*

Mississippi was in many ways a time capsule. So much of the sameness
that dominated America hadn't dawned on the Delta.
Ace Atkins, *Crossroad Blues*

...deswamped and denuded and derivered.
William Faulkner, *Go Down, Moses*, description of the Delta

Things get weird as shit in the Delta.
Doug Roberts

The Delta contains lots of eccentrics, boozers, and nutballs.
Doug Roberts

Drugs, religion, and welfare appeared to be
the cornerstones of the Delta economy.
Richard Grant, *Dispatches from Pluto*

Everywhere life is teeming, fighting, killing, dying, rotting, breeding,
gorging itself on the riches of the Delta's biomass.
Richard Grant, *Dispatches from Pluto*

It was all so familiar from Latin America, Africa, and the Caribbean:
the collapsing infrastructure, the intermittent electricity supply,
the air of lassitude and disorganization.
Richard Grant, *Dispatches from Pluto*

The Mississippi Delta — the South's South.
Common saying

People needed tools to cope with all the poverty, tragedy, and
dysfunction in the Delta, and the most popular ones were denial,
religion, gallows humor, drugs, and alcohol.
Richard Grant, *Dispatches from Pluto*

This was a typical Delta story... it contained mischief, alcohol, clever
whimsical use of language, and the humiliation of a tight-assed
authority figure. As such, it was also typical
of a story you might hear in Ireland.
Richard Grant, *Dispatches from Pluto*

I have seen children in the Delta of Mississippi with distended
stomachs, whose faces are covered with sores from starvation... I
don't think that's acceptable in the United States
of America and we need a change.
Senator Robert Kennedy, on poverty in the Mississippi Delta

There was certainly a psychic transformation one felt when
transitioning from the Delta to the hills. It gets colder for one thing.
And there's less unbridled looniness.
Jim Dees, *The Statue & the Fury*

DOGS

You should be ashamed not to own a dog, and so should
everybody else who doesn't own a dog.
William Faulkner

My dog has a number of acquaintances... but there is little company in
the world which we enjoy as much as each other's.
Donna Tartt

A man's dog don't care whether he's rich or po'.
Holt Collier

I don't trust a man that doesn't love a dog.
William Faulkner

In New York, even the dogs look inhuman.
William Faulkner, remark to columnist Rhea Talley

He will need to be a little bigger than smart,
and a little braver than either.
William Faulkner, *Go Down, Moses*, Sam Father on small fyce dog

...he is as cogent as a bird dog quartering a field.
Walker Percy, *The Moviegoer*

The latest conundrum: how to keep the dogs from getting into your
trash cans. Because your lazy husband forgets to put it out on the right
pick-up day. 'Just pour some pneumonia in that garbage.
Dogs won't so much as wink at them cans.'
Kathryn Stockett, *The Help*

The dog of your boyhood teaches you a great deal about friendship,
and love, and death: old Skip was my brother. They had buried him
under our elm tree... yet this wasn't totally true.
For he really lay buried in my heart.
Willie Morris

Banjo was a champion when it came to having heart.
Marshall Ramsey, on his dog Banjo

Sometimes you don't find a dog. Sometimes the dog finds you.
Marshall Ramsey, *Chainsaws & Casseroles*

Felt no mercy lately? Touch a dog's ears.
Barry Hannah

(My dog Holly) is not afraid of the devil, large dogs, or the laundryman.
I can't speak for the devil and large dogs, but the
laundryman is afraid of her.
Charlotte Capers, *The Capers Papers*

DRINKING

It requires long training to drink really hard, and the training runs
counter to the requirements of most of the other endurance sports.
Jack Butler, *Jujitsu for Christ*

...always good company — if she keeps the drinking under control and
doesn't set fire to the house.
Ellen Douglas

Which I ain't got nothing against a man
drinking in the morning if he want to.
Larry Brown, *Dirty Work*

Blanche: ...put the bottle away so I won't be tempted.
Tennessee Williams, *A Streetcar Named Desire*

Stanley: Some people rarely touch it, but it touches them
often.
Tennessee Williams, *A Streetcar Named Desire*, on liquor

Stella: When men are drinking and playing poker, anything
can happen.
Tennessee Williams, *A Streetcar Named Desire*

Stella: She and Steve had a row. Has she got the police?
Stanley: Naw. She's gettin' a drink.
Stella: That's much more practical!
Tennessee Williams, *A Streetcar Named Desire*

Not only is my date inexplicably rude, but drop-dead drunk.
Kathryn Stockett, *The Help*

You got nothing left here but enemies in the Junior League and a mama
that's gone drive you to drink. You done burned ever bridge there is.
Kathryn Stockett, *The Help*

Quittin' work, devoting yourself to the occupation of drinkin'.
Tennessee Williams, *Cat on a Hot Tin Roof*

Mendacity is a system that we live in. Liquor is one
way out and death's the other.
Tennessee Williams, *Cat on a Hot Tin Roof*

That's the truth. I never trusted a man that didn't drink.
Tennesse Williams, *Cat on a Hot Tin Roof*

Mr. Lockhair, a man generally respected by his neighbors while sober,
was killed by his own son.
Mississippian newspaper, 1854

The Episcopalian ideal of a gentleman is a man who, if a lady falls
down drunk, will pick her up off the floor and freshen up her drink.
Gayden Metcalfe, *Being Dead Is No Excuse*

If, when you say whiskey, you mean the devil's brew, the poison scourge,
the bloody monster that defiles innocence, dethrones reason, destroys
the home, creates misery and poverty, yea, literally takes the bread from
the mouths of little children… then certainly I am against it. But if,
when you say whiskey, you mean the oil of conversation, the
philosophic wine… the drink which enables a man to magnify his joy;
if you mean the drink the sale of which pours into our treasuries
untold millions of dollars to provide tender care for our
little crippled children… then certainly I am for it.
Soggy Sweat, excerpt from "The Whiskey Speech"

Likker ain't nothin' to play 'round with, get
you in trouble faster'n anything I know of.
Armis Hawkins, *The Grand Leader*

Likker and bad company are dynamite.
Armis Hawkins, *The Grand Leader*

Kelsie Kinsmore's a man I wouldn't take no drink
with even ef that sonabitch drank.
Armis Hawkins, *The Grand Leader*

The tools I need for my trade are paper,
tobacco, food, and a little whiskey.
William Faulkner

He knows every cuss word in the dictionary, every poker hand in the deck, and every whiskey label in the distillery.
William Faulkner, *Race At Morning*

William Faulkner: I took up a rotary-motored Spad with a crock of bourbon in the cockpit, gave diligent attention to both, and executed… part of what could easily have turned out to be a nearly perfect loop.
John Faulkner: What do you mean, part of a loop?
William Faulkner: That's what it was; a hangar got in the way, and I flew through the roof and ended up hanging on the rafters.

There's a lot of nourishment in an acre of corn.
William Faulkner, on whiskey

Don't you ever let me catch you giving that child whiskey again — without sugar.
William Faulkner's grandmother upbraiding her husband

In those days (before becoming a novelist), I was a free man. Had one pair of pants, one pair of shoes, and an old trench coat with a pocket big enough for a whiskey bottle. Now I get stacks of letters asking what I eat for breakfast.
William Faulkner

Anybody who can sell a book to the movies for $50,000 has a right to get drunk and dance in his bare feet.
William Faulkner, on selling movie rights to *Intruder in the Dust*

I went to school at Virginia. Teach you how to drink there.
William Faulkner, *Sanctuary*

It's a good thing that in a changing world there are some unchanging things you can count on, like the quality of Jack Daniels.
William Faulkner

I'll never feel comfortable taking a strong drink, and I'll never feel easy smoking a cigarette. I just don't think those things are right for me.
Elvis Presley

The wild stuff is overrated. Drinking, you don't feel good all the time. There's a lot of down, a lot of misery.

Barry Hannah

The first two drinks were always wonderfully liberating. You think better. You're braver, and you'll say anything. If you could just hang in there with two or three, it'd be beautiful. The trouble was, I couldn't.

Barry Hannah

It's been six years since I had a drink. I have two girls, and my priorities are a lot different now. I just can't believe I was that guy. I would not go back. I would not trade the way I am now for anything.

Brett Favre

Half of those eight or nine years, I don't even remember.

Brett Favre

A lot of people didn't know how to drive drunk, and they were the ones who caused all the wrecks.

Larry Brown, *Father and Son*

A thirty-ish, dark-haired reporter wearing a Palm Beach suit and a drooping mustache, who looked too hung over to object to my presence.

Tim Crouse, *The Boys on the Bus*, on Curtis Wilkie

Moonshine flourished more readily than cotton.

Curtis Wilkie, *George Magazine*

They took away our zip code, because we ran out of people and the postmistress drank too much.

Martha Foose, on her hometown

…in the Mississippi Delta… some folks could barely conceive of going down the road without a beer or a traveler. As one man explained to me, 'You never know what's going to happen, especially at night. You might end up in a ditch and damn sure need a drink of whiskey.'

Richard Grant, *Dispatches from Pluto*

Drinking and fighting are accepted and often respected social
endeavors, and defending one's honor is still considered
worthy if not mandatory.
Stuart Stevens, *The Daily Beast*

...drinking would begin around 10:00 in the morning, which isn't a
terrible thing, but it did take some combination of
practice and natural ability.
Stuart Stevens, *The Last Season*

Between Scotch and nothing, I'll take Scotch.
William Faulkner, who was a bourbon man

Neshoba was one of the wettest counties in the dry state of Mississippi.
Florence Mars

Thou shalt not drink.
Bible Belt Mississippi's Eleventh Commandment

Ezra Brooks has been mighty kind to me. I don't see how I can let him
down in his hour of need. Case dismissed.
Judge George Adams invoking his favorite whiskey in a case
brought by citizens opposed to liquor

I can't drink at all. One drink is too many and a thousand's not enough.
Donna Tartt, *The Goldfinch*

I was put in charge of getting Willie Morris and James Dickey to a
series of television interviews. They started drinking early as we traveled
from station to station. At the last stop the station manager said to me,
'Do you know that these men are drunk?' I replied, 'Yes, and
furthermore if you don't give them another drink, they
will not go on your show.'
Winston Groom

The first question a person from the hills asks when they meet someone
new is what church do you go to. Down in the Delta the first thing we
ask is what whiskey do you drink. And then we know
what church you go to.
Judge Allen Pepper

EDUCATION

Education is to economic development what fertilizer is to farming.
Jack Reed

The road out of the poor house runs past the school house.
Governor William Winter

Mississippi's 1982 Education Reform Act was the most important civil
rights, economic development, and national security
legislation passed in 1982.
Carl Rowan, nationally syndicated columnist

We should pay our teachers as if our children's lives
depend on it, because they do.
Governor Ray Mabus

Far more educated than any people in history, we
are uncertain of what we can believe in.
Wyatt Cooper, *Families*

As with all great teachers, his curriculum was an insignificant part of
what he communicated. From him you didn't learn a subject, but a
life.… Tolerance and justice, fearlessness and pride, reverence and pity,
are learned in a course on long division if the
teacher has those qualities.
William Alexander Percy

They didn't give you much schooling because just as soon as you was
big enough, you get to working in the fields.
Muddy Waters

Life deals you lots of lessons. Some people
learn from it; some people don't.
Brett Favre

The beautiful thing about learning is nobody can take it away from you.
B.B. King

The gift represents a transfer of wealth from people on the cutting edge of society to people who are struggling just to get started.

New York Times, on Jim Barksdale's $100 million
contribution to fight illiteracy in Mississippi

We can do this. God did not draw a line around Mississippi and say, 'Your children will have less opportunity.' We have the potential to lead this country in education. All we have to have is the will.

Governor Ray Mabus

Got some discount knowledge at the junior college
where we majored in beer and girls.

Rivers Rutherford, "These Are My People"

Poorly educated people translate into poor people. Education is the one thing that will break the cycle of poverty. Education is the only thing that will unlock the door of economic opportunity.

Governor William Winter

…April was the best, the very best time of all not to have to go to school, until you would think, 'Except in the fall,' with the weather brisk and not-cold at the same time and trees all yellow and red and you could go hunting all day long; and then you would think, 'Except in the winter,' with the Christmas holidays over and now nothing to look forward to until summer; and you would think how no time is the best time to not have to go to school, and so school is a good thing after all, because without it there wouldn't be any holidays or vacations.

William Faulkner, *The Town*

I learned in spite of the instructors we had. They were a bunch of broken-down preachers: head full of dogma and intolerance and a belly full of meaningless words… But in spite of it, I kind of got interested in learning things.

William Faulkner, *Mosquitos*

I have never lectured; I can't lecture, and I won't lecture.

William Faulkner to Ole Miss English class

What we need in Mississippi is the best possible schools, to make the best possible use of the men and women we produce, regardless of what color they are.

William Faulkner

I feel that for one who did not even graduate from grammar school, to accept an honorary degree representative, not only of higher learning, but of post-graduate labor in it, would debase and nullify the whole aim of learning.

William Faulkner, declining an honorary degree from Tulane University

I read to learn what I learned.

William Faulkner, on reading great literature

We Mississippians already know that our present schools are not good enough.

William Faulkner, letter to the Memphis *Commercial Appeal*, 1955

I have no degrees nor diplomas from any school. I am an old veteran sixth grader. Maybe that's why I have so much respect for education that I seem unable to sit quiet and watch it held subordinate to an emotional state concerning the color of human skin.

William Faulkner

'Dream of Pines' was the best high school band in at least the world.

Barry Hannah, *Geronimo Rex*

There were twenty (teachers) actively, passively, strangely, cryptically, feverishly incoherent, each in his own special style.

Barry Hannah, *Geronimo Rex*

This (college) is no place for me for another half hour, let alone two years.

Walker Percy, *The Last Gentleman*

I never cared what kind of grade I got.

Shelby Foote

This is a university. It's not a shrine for the preservation of the relics of the Civil War.

Ole Miss Student Union President

Good schools don't just happen and certainly don't happen overnight; they are built and rebuilt by loving critics, and it takes time.

Andy Mullins

Teachers will come in believing you will save the world, so don't get
discouraged when you find, at the end of your first year, that you have
only saved one student. That is plenty sufficient to
come back for another year.

Andy Mullins

It's just as impossible for me to imagine that fear could stand in the way
of the education I want as it is for me to imagine
not wanting the education.

James Meredith

The fault begins with the Boys of Spring, whose principal problem
seems to be how to keep out of each other's way.

Senator Ellis Bodron, blaming the effort to pass kindergartens
in Mississippi on Governor William Winter's young staff

Sonny Montgomery's legacy is the Montgomery GI Bill, which
provided upward mobility to American veterans willing to work after
their military service was complete. It can be said with clarity that
perhaps no single American did more to help middle-class and poor
Americans attain a college education than this humble,
dignified citizen soldier from Mississippi.

Sid Salter

ENDURANCE

Man is stronger and tougher and more enduring
than even his mistakes and blundering.
William Faulkner, *To the Youth of Japan*

Once you fully apprehend the vacuity of a life without struggle, you are
equipped with the basic means of salvation.
Tennessee Williams

They endured.
William Faulkner, *The Sound and the Fury*

I can bear anything.
William Faulkner

…theirs was an armament which the white man could not match nor –
if he but knew it – even cope with: patience.
William Faulkner, *Intruder in the Dust*

It would be there… tomorrow and tomorrow and tomorrow — not
only to hope, not even to wait: just to endure.
William Faulkner, *Pylon*

I find the world sufferable.
Beth Ann Fennelly, *Say You Waved: A Dream Song Cycle*

The violets in the mountains have broken the rocks.
Tennessee Williams

EVIL

…a common evil — the defiling of the proud human spirit.
Eudora Welty, *The House of Willa Cather*

We must just stay awake and see evil done for a little while.
William Faulkner, *The Sound and the Fury*

Between nothing and evil, I will take nothing.
William Faulkner, *A Fable*

The evil prosper, and the innocent pay the bills for them.
Greg Iles, *Natchez Burning*

Greed, apathy, hubris — even loyalty — all demand payment in the
end. Storms will always come, and men will always do evil in
the shadow of some other word.
Greg Iles, *The Bone Tree*

Treachery, weakness, envy, fanaticism — the most
destructive forces available to man.
Greg Iles, *Spandau Phoenix*

They understand not only evil, it seemed, but the extravagance
of tricks with which evil presents itself as good.
Donna Tartt, *The Secret History*

FAILURE

Maybe it's just as well that we are doomed to fail, since, as long as we do fail as the hand continues to hold blood, we will try again…

William Faulkner, remarks upon receiving The National Book Award for Fiction

…there are all sorts of persons in families… There was usually the one who played around, the one who always lost his job, the one who gossiped, the one who got rich, the one who got religion, the one who drank, and at least one who was just plain bad.

Wyatt Cooper, *Families*

Failure is another stepping stone to greatness.

Oprah Winfrey

Even failure is worthwhile and admirable, provided only that the failure is splendid enough…

William Faulkner, remarks upon receiving National Book Award for Fiction

Failure brings me stimulation to try to do better in each new book.

William Faulkner

All of us failed to match our dreams of perfection. So I rate us on the basis of our splendid failure to do the impossible.

William Faulkner

We all had better grieve for all people beneath a culture which holds any mechanical instrument superior to any man simply because the one, being mechanical, is infallible, while the other, being nothing but man, is not just subject to failure, but doomed to it.

William Faulkner, letter to the *New York Times*

I don't believe in failure. It is not failure if you enjoyed the process.

Oprah Winfrey

Go ahead. Fall down. The world looks different from the ground.

Oprah Winfrey

FARMING

We had about fifty-five cows which was fifty-four too many.
Joe Wood, Mississippi high school football coach

I am a farmer this time of year; up until he sells his crops, no Mississippi farmer has the time or money either to travel anywhere on.
William Faulkner, letter to Mark Van Doren

I won't be able to come to receive the prize myself. It's too far away. I am a farmer down here, and I can't get away.
William Faulkner, on winning the Nobel Prize, to journalist Sven Ahman

...the long, monotonous, endless, unendable furrows of Mississippi cotton fields.
William Faulkner, *Requiem For a Nun*

...the land provided our total living. We lived on it... with independence and self-reliance and pride.
Wyatt Cooper, father of CNN's Anderson Cooper, *Families*

One rain won't make a crop.
Earnestine Moore

The good farmer gets acquainted with the daybreak.
Earnestine Moore

The rooster makes more racket than the hen that laid the egg.
Earnestine Moore

Corn and crow can't grow in the same field.
Earnestine Moore

FAULKNER'S YOKNAPATAWPHA COUNTY

Beat Four – the most remote, fierce, and intractable
of the five beats of Yoknapatawpha County.
Joseph Blotner

Beat Four already in advance didn't like most of
the things which people from town did.
William Faulkner, *Intruder in the Dust*

The only stranger to enter with impunity was God,
and He only by daylight and on Sunday.
William Faulkner, *Intruder in the Dust*, describing Beat Four

…that whole region of lonely pine hills dotted meagerly with small
tilted farms and peripatetic sawmills and contraband whiskey kettles,
where peace officers from town didn't even go
unless they were sent for…
William Faulkner, *Intruder in the Dust*

…a different kind of Snopes like a cotton-mouth
is a different kind of snake.
William Faulkner

…Our folklore, or Snopeslore, if you like.
William Faulkner, *The Town*

By the beginning of the twentieth century, Snopeses were everywhere;
not only behind the counters of grubbing little side street stores…
but behind the president's desks of banks… and in
the deaconries of Baptist churches.
William Faulkner, Essay on Mississippi

Ain't there souls turning up here every day, banging at the door and
raising all kinds of hell to get in here, even bring letters
from Congressmen that we never heard of?
William Faulkner, *The Hamlet*, the Prince of Hell on Flem Snopes

...the gradual eating-up of Jefferson by Snopeses, who corrupt the local government with crooked politics, buy up all the colonial homes and tear them down and chop up the lots into subdivisions.

William Faulkner to Bob Haas

The court disagrees with Sony's characterization of *Requiem* as being "relatively obscure." Nothing in the Yoknapatawpha canon is obscure. Having viewed the two works at issue in this case, the court is convinced that one is timeless, the other temporal.

Opinion by **U.S. District Judge Mike Mills** in case pitting the Faulkner estate against Woody Allen and Sony Pictures

I'm a Yoknapatawphanatic.

Eudora Welty

FEAR

The basest of all things is to be afraid.
William Faulkner, Nobel Prize address

Our danger is the forces in the world today which are trying to use
man's fear to rob him of his individuality, his soul… giving him free
food which he has not earned, easy and valueless money
which he has not worked for.
William Faulkner, Nobel Prize address

Never be afraid to raise your voice for honesty and truth and
compassion, against injustice and lying and greed.
William Faulkner, address to University High School

Our ancestors were not afraid — our grandfathers who fought at First
and Second Manassas and Sharpsburg and Shiloh and Franklin and
Chickamauga and Chancellorsville and The Wilderness; let alone
those who survived that and had the even greater courage
and endurance to resist and survive Reconstruction.
William Faulkner

…the mind is afraid of fire.
William Faulkner, letter to Joan Williams

The brave man is not he who does not know fear; the brave man is he
who says to himself, 'I am afraid. I will decide quickly
what to do, and then I will do it.'
William Faulkner, letter to Jimmy Faulkner in 1943

…thinking it into words even only to himself was like the struck match
which doesn't dispel the dark, but only exposes its terror.
William Faulkner, *Intruder in the Dust*

I'm scared to death of horses. That's why I can't leave them alone.
William Faulkner

It always sound scarier when a hollerer talk soft.
Kathryn Stockett, *The Help*

The older I get, the more things scare me.
Richard Ford, *The Sportswriter*

Alice Hunt's… big fear is ending up in the new part of the cemetery where, she says, she doesn't know a soul.
Gayden Metcalfe, *Being Dead Is No Excuse*

That was the way he lived: he passed his days trying to defeat or gratify powerful impulses in a world he feared.
Richard Wright, *Native Son*

I have a lot of things to prove to myself. One is that I can live my life fearlessly.
Oprah Winfrey

The thing you fear most has no power. Your fear of it is what has the power. Facing the truth really will set you free.
Oprah Winfrey

But fear and danger aren't always directly proportional. We're all terrified by rattlesnakes, but the spider we brush off our sleeve with hardly a thought is far more likely to hurt us.
Greg Iles, *Natchez Burning*

It's odd how our fears, the ones we didn't know we had, alter our sight line and make us see things that never were.
Richard Ford, *The Lay of the Land*

Make friends with fear… because it will not go away, and it will destroy you if left uncontrolled.
John Grisham, *A Time to Kill*

It was okay to be afraid - just don't show it.
John Grisham, *A Time to Kill*

FOOTBALL

When he describes a goal-line stand against LSU in 1932, it is
like King Arthur standing fast in the blood-red sunset
against Sir Mordred and the traitors.

Walker Percy, *The Moviegoer*

When we thought about football, which was
every day, we thought about LSU.

Robert Khayat, *The Education of a Lifetime*

Keep going, keep going. Fight for more yards.

Walter Payton

With the game on the line, I want the ball in my hands.

Eli Manning

Every game I've ever played, regardless if it was pre-season or Super
Bowl, meant the same to me. I laid it all on the line.

Brett Favre

Dammit, if I'd known that son of a bitch was going to run it
back for a touchdown, I'd have punted it out of bounds.

Jake Gibbs, who punted to Billy Cannon in the famed 1959 Ole Miss vs. LSU game

You can do anything for two weeks. Heck, you can
stack greased BBs for two weeks.

Ackerman High School football coach, on two-a-day practices in the August heat

Little Wide Load… was a fullback, but what he really liked to do was
run into people. He had the longest unofficial run in Ole Miss history,
147 yards, when he had picked up a fumbled snap in the end-zone just
before he went out of bounds and proceeded to run over every tackler
on the Tennessee team except one, and he was chasing that one
into the stands when he slipped and fell.

Jack Butler, *Jujitsu for Christ*

The Alabama team is still whipping everybody in sight.

Barry Hannah, *Ray*

Being smart on the football team meant that you read
Time magazine and had heard of the Marshall Plan.
Walker Percy, *Lancelot*

Archie who?
Dismissive comment by **Univ. of Tennessee linebacker Steve Kiner**,
which inflamed the Ole Miss football team and led to the defeat of
number one-ranked Tennessee by Ole Miss.

It's not fair for a guy to be six foot, three inches, 233 pounds, have 9.5
speed, and know karate too.
Coach Barry Switzer on Marcus Dupree

How'd you make straight A's and play football? I put the books first.
John Grisham, *The Firm*

When you lose a family member or something tragic happens, that stays
with you forever… Football is important, but not as
important as you once thought it was.
Brett Favre

When I wasn't in the Super Bowl, I wished I was.
Brett Favre

I consider adversity being good sometimes.
Brett Favre

I'm the best Manning.
Peyton Manning

My dad told us up front, 'Guys, if you want to play sports,
go ahead. But it's your decision.'
Peyton Manning

Whenever I took a false step or two, I felt the consequences.
Peyton Manning

You hear about how many fourth-quarter comebacks that a guy has,
and I think it means a guy screwed up in the first three quarters.
Peyton Manning

The good news is the score is always zero-zero
when you kick off the next week.
Archie Manning, on losing

Most coaches say the same things over and over. Probably 20
guys on the team could give his speech for him.
Archie Manning

I'm very excited for them. I can tell you for sure it's exciting because in
my 15 years, this time of year I was packing up my stuff to go home.
Archie Manning, on Peyton and Eli making it to the playoffs

I wish I'd played my whole career in flag football.
Archie Manning

I wish I'd never touched a football.
Bobby Crespino, standout receiver at Ole Miss and the NFL.
He ended up suffering from severe dementia from hits and concussions.

The coaches were unreasonably tough… We weren't sure if they were
trying to make us the best players possible or if they
were trying to send us back home.
Robert Khayat, *The Education of a Lifetime*

Get up, son! My hemorrhoids bleed more than that every morning.
Ole Miss football coach to injured and bleeding player

He was about as erotic as an old football coach.
Donna Tartt, *The Secret History*

We listened to the Ole Miss coaches yell at their players. A team could
be up by one hundred points, and coaches would still yell.
Stuart Stevens, *The Last Season*

From the time I hit high school, girls had
become more important than football.
Stuart Stevens, *The Last Season*

You can't join a team and give up on it because you
lose a few games or things aren't going well.
Eli Manning

It's the only way I've played sports and done things. I'm
low-key, but I'm very competitive and hate to lose.
Eli Manning

I don't like the feeling of losing.
Eli Manning

FREEDOM

Man's hope is in man's freedom.
William Faulkner, *To the Youth of Japan*

...liberty gained without honor and sacrifice and held without constant vigilance and undiminished honor and complete willingness to sacrifice again at need, was not worth having to begin with.
William Faulkner, *An Innocent at Rinkside*

...that simple belief of man that he can be free — is the strongest force on Earth, and all we need to do is use it.
William Faulkner, address to the Southern Historical Association

...that simple belief of individual man that he can and should and will be free.
William Faulkner

We must be free not because we claim freedom, but because we practice it.
William Faulkner, address to the Southern Historical Association

Man is free, and he is responsible, terribly responsible.
William Faulkner to Loic Bourvard

You're itching for freedom, but you won't scratch.
Mississippi Minister to 1963 NAACP Rally

Books were my pass to personal freedom. I learned to read at age three and soon discovered there was a whole world to conquer that went beyond our farm in Mississippi.
Oprah Winfrey

To be free is to have achieved your life.
Tennessee Williams

Today less than one percent of the country wears the uniform... It's dangerous in a democracy when there's too much distance between those who are doing the protecting and those who are protected.
Secretary of the Navy Ray Mabus

Freedom is a helluva lot more terrifying than any prison.
Neil White, "Lepers & Cons"

FRIENDSHIP

What's friendship's realest measure? I'll tell you. The amount of precious time you'll squander on someone else's calamities and fuckups.
Richard Ford, *The Sportswriter*

Bilbo stuck to his friends, no matter how reprehensible they might be.
J.P. Coleman

She is the mother I never had; she is the sister everybody would want. She is the friend that everybody deserves. I don't know a better person.
Oprah Winfrey

Life is partly what we make it, and partly
what it is made by the friends we choose.
Tennessee Williams

...friendship really has love in it.... It is an essential part of your life.
Eudora Welty

For a moment there I thought you were testing our friendship.
Eudora Welty to Bill Ferris, thinking Ferris had suggested a 7:30 a.m. meeting

THE GREAT DEPRESSION

What do such numbers mean? How can anguish and
hunger be graphed?

Robert McElvaine, *Down and Out in the Great Depression*

Please help us if you can.

Letter from anonymous black resident of Picayune,
Mississippi, to President Franklin Roosevelt

I have not got anything for security but my honor.

Letter from Tupelo woman to FDR, 1935

You couldn't find a dollar with a search warrant in those days.

J.P. Coleman on the Great Depression

I prize the Depression because I learned the value of things in the
Depression in a way that people who don't have to worry about
such things never learned to prize it, really.

Shelby Foote

HISTORY

The past is never dead. It's not even past.
William Faulkner, *Requiem for a Nun*

Einstein said the arrow of time flies in only one direction. Faulkner,
being from Mississippi, understood the matter differently. He said the
past is never dead; it's not even past. All of us labor in webs spun
long before we were born, webs of heredity and environment,
of desire and consequence, of history and eternity.
Greg Iles, *The Quiet Game*

Trying to keep the past buried was like
trying to stop kudzu from growing.
Greg Iles, *Natchez Burning*

…I felt the dry itch of the past rubbing against the present.
Greg Iles, *Dead Sleep*

Our actions have consequences that last long after us, entwining the
present with the future in ways we cannot begin to understand.
Greg Iles, *The Quiet Game*

The light of long ago is different from the light of today, and yet here,
in this house, I'm reminded of the past at every turn.
Donna Tartt, *The Goldfinch*

How strange to find that the present contained such a bright shard of
the living past, damaged and eroded, but not destroyed.
Donna Tartt, *The Goldfinch*

Ours is the only civilization in history which has enshrined
mediocrity as its national ideal. Others have been corrupt, but leave it
to us to invent the most undistinguished of corruptions. No orgies, no
blood running in the street, no babies thrown off cliffs. No, we
are a sentimental people and horrify easily.
Walker Percy, *The Moviegoer*

...you — everyone — must, or anyway may have to, pay for your past: the past is something like a promissory note with a trick clause in it which, as long as nothing goes wrong, can be manumitted in an orderly manner, but which fate or luck or chance can foreclose on you without warning.

William Faulkner, *Requiem for a Nun*

HUMAN NATURE

…he wished he were more of what he wasn't and less of what he was.
Paige Mitchell, *A Wilderness of Monkeys*

Sometimes a man has to believe in his
mistakes as well as his achievements.
Paige Mitchell, *A Wilderness of Monkeys*

Sometimes, we, in the middle of our lives, are so confused and bogged
down in the details of living that we've forgotten the ideals we began
with or the wisdom we're looking forward to.
Paige Mitchell, *A Wilderness of Monkeys*

God made us different and we should love His
differences as well as His likenesses.
Barry Hannah, *Airships*, "Knowing He Was Not My Kind"

At the great moments of life — success, failure, marriage, death — our
kind of folks have always possessed a native instinct for… grace.
Walker Percy, *The Moviegoer*

Surely it is the highest tribute to the best people we know to use them as
best we can, to become, not their disciples, but ourselves.
Walker Percy, Introduction to *Lanterns on the Levee*

…for the past few years I had done nothing but fiddle at law, fiddle at
history, keep up with the news (why?), watch *Mary Tyler Moore* and drink
myself into unconsciousness every night.
Walker Percy, *Lancelot*

What a bog and labyrinth the human essence is… We are
all overbrained and overemotioned.
Barry Hannah

…time is short and it doesn't return again. It is slipping while I write
this and while you read it, and the monosyllable of the clock is Loss,
Loss, Loss, unless you devote your heart to its opposition.
Tennessee Williams

Blanche: There's so much confusion in the world.

Tennessee Williams, *A Streetcar Named Desire*

'Are you happy, Minny?'
'Course I's happy. You happy too. Big house, big yard, husband looking
after you.' I frown at Miss Celia and I make sure she can see it. Because
ain't that white people for you, wondering if they are happy enough.

Kathryn Stockett, *The Help*

Ever morning, until you dead in the ground, you gone have to make
this decision. You gone have to ask yourself, 'Am I gone
believe what them fools say about me today?'

Kathryn Stockett, *The Help*

Everyone's asleep in this town in every way possible.

Kathryn Stockett, *The Help*

I've had a secret joy and a secret dread both rattling inside a me.

Kathryn Stockett, *The Help*

Welcome to Carville, where they quarantine lepers, where the
petrochemical companies discharge their waste, and where they send
the likes of us. You're now officially part of a human garbage dump.

Neil White, *In the Sanctuary of Outcasts*

Neil White: I wanted everyone to think I was perfect.
Ella Bounds: Well, you ain't gotta worry about that no more.

Neil White, *In the Sanctuary of Outcasts*

I went to sleep with the most terrible visions of imminent failure.

Willie Morris, *North Toward Home*, describing the
night before his Rhodes Scholarship interview

When you got what I got, you do one of two things. You either blow
your head off with a shotgun or you become a Christian.

Rae Morris while dying of cancer, to his son Willie Morris

I'm not living with you. We occupy the same cage.

Tennessee Williams, *Cat on a Hot Tin Roof*

When you are sixteen, you do not know what your parents know, or much of what they understand, and less of what's in their hearts.
Richard Ford, *Wildlife*

Sometimes you have to do the wrong thing just to know you're alive.
Richard Ford, *Wildlife*

People were drawn to things they shouldn't be.
Richard Ford, *Wildlife*

I looked out my window, stood in my yard, watched sunsets with a sense of solace and achievement, cleaned my rain gutters, eyed my shingles, put up storms, fertilized regularly, computed my equity, spoke to my neighbors in an interested voice — the normal applauseless life of us all.
Richard Ford, *The Sportswriter*

Misery does not want company — happiness does.
Richard Ford, *The Sportswriter*

Deep down we're all reaching out for a decent rewarding contact every chance we get.
Richard Ford, *The Sportswriter*

Don't be too hard on yourself. Now and again it's okay to let yourself off the hook.
Tom Franklin, *Crooked Letter, Crooked Letter*

Some of the damndest fool things ever been did was by folks with good intentions.
Armis Hawkins, *The Grand Leader*

Adversity is sometimes hard upon a man, but for one man who can stand prosperity, there are a hundred that will stand adversity.
Elvis Presley

The image is one thing and the human being is another. It's very hard to live up to an image.
Elvis Presley

I'm trying to keep a level head. You have to be careful out in
the world. It's so easy to get turned.
Elvis Presley

It's human nature to gripe, but I'm going
ahead and doing the best I can.
Elvis Presley

I don't think I'm bad for people. If I did think I was bad for
people, I would go back to driving a truck.
Elvis Presley

I'm black. It's part of who I am. It does not define me.
Oprah Winfrey

We have to distrust each other. It's our only defense against betrayal.
Tennessee Williams

It would be inexcusably selfish to be lonely alone.
Tennessee Williams

I have found it easier to identify with characters who verge upon hysteria, were frightened of life, who were desperate to reach out to another
person. But these seemingly fragile people are the strong people, really.
Tennessee Williams

All cruel people describe themselves as paragons of frankness.
Tennessee Williams

I think most of us are disturbed.
Tennessee Williams

Humanity is just a work in progress.
Tennessee Williams

Leaving reminds us of what we can part with and what we can't, then
offers us something new to look forward to, to dream about.
Richard Ford

Of all the passions of mankind, the love of novelty most rules the mind. In search of this, from realm to realm we roam. Our fleets come loaded with every folly home.

Shelby Foote

I need to draw closer… to gather the older generations with the younger.

Sela Ward, *Homesick*

Mrs. Ford's love of animals was matched only by her disdain for most humans.

Robert Khayat, *The Education of a Lifetime*

We are always looking for absolutes and not finding them.

Richard Ford, *Wildlife*

Be kind to me… I know it will make everything better.

Richard Ford, *Wildlife*

There are no degrees of best; one man's best is the equal of any other best.

William Faulkner, address to American Academy of Arts and Letters

Man does not seem to be able to stand very much prosperity… Defeat is good for him.

William Faulkner

…one universe, one cosmos… the very substance in which he lives, and lacking which, he would vanish in a matter of seconds — is murmurous with his fears and terrors and disclaimers and repudiations and his aspirations and dreams and his baseless hopes, bouncing back at him in radar waves from the constellations.

William Faulkner, *Requiem for a Nun*

All men are equal on one score; all suffer the same anguish and pain.

William Faulkner

…man's hope and aspirations which have enabled him to prevail above his condition and fate and his own self-created disasters.

William Faulkner

Human beings are terrible. One must believe well in man to endure
him, wait out his folly and savagery and inhumanity.
William Faulkner, letter to Else Jonsson

There aren't any morals. People just do the best they can.
William Faulkner, *The Mansion*

The last sound on the worthless earth will be two human beings
trying to launch a homemade space ship and already
quarreling about where they are going next.
William Faulkner, speech to UNESCO

I like to think anyone grows as he gets older... he prefers to believe he
understands more. He's not always able to forgive human folly,
but he is able to understand it.
William Faulkner, remarks to Balch Lecture

No man can cause more grief than that one
clinging blindly to the vices of his ancestors.
William Faulkner, *Intruder in the Dust*

...a blending of anger and shame and
shame at being angry and ashamed.
William Faulkner, *Intruder in the Dust*

...people named Gowrie and McCallum and Fraser and Ingrum...
who love brawling and fear God and believe in Hell.
William Faulkner, *Intruder in the Dust*

...if you would peruse in unbroken — nay, overlapping — continuity
the history of a community, look not in the church registers and courthouse records, but beneath the successive layers of calcimine and cre-
osote and white wash on the walls of the jail, since only in that forcible
carceration does man find the idleness in which to compose, in the gross
and simple terms of his gross and simple lusts and yearnings, the gross
and simple recapitulations of his gross and simple heart.
William Faulkner, *Requiem for a Nun*

The terrible truth is that brutality is part of human nature, and all the laws in the world can't neuter it.

Greg Iles, *The Devil's Punchbowl*

If a man lived long enough, his past would always overtake him, no matter how fast he ran or how morally he tried to live subsequently. And how men dealt with that law ultimately revealed their true natures.

Greg Iles, *Natchez Burning*

What if one is possessed of a heart that can't be trusted? What if the heart, for its own unfathomable reasons, leads one willfully and in a cloud of unspeakable radiance away from health, domesticity, civic responsibility and strong social connections and all the blandly held common virtues and instead straight toward a beautiful flare of ruin, self-immolation, disaster?

Donna Tartt, *The Goldfinch*

Sometimes we want what we want, even if we know it's going to kill us.

Donna Tartt, *The Goldfinch*

What if our badness and mistakes are the very thing that set our fate and bring us round to good? What if, for some of us, we can't get there any other way?

Donna Tartt, *The Goldfinch*

…no person, no matter how beloved, can ever truly understand us.

Donna Tartt, *The Secret History*

The Greeks… knew how foolish it was to deny the unseen world, the old gods. Emotion, darkness, barbarism.

Donna Tartt, *The Secret History*

I began somewhere along the line to mistrust the expertness of experts.

Wyatt Cooper, *Families*

He sure found out the hard way
That dreams don't always come true.

Jim Weatherly, "Midnight Train to Georgia"

...Virgil gave a sigh, as if he knew that when you go looking
for what is lost, everything is a sign.
Eudora Welty, *The Collected Stories*

People are mostly layers of violence and tenderness wrapped like bulbs,
and it is difficult to say what makes them onions or hyacinths.
Eudora Welty

If you don't plant the seed, it doesn't matter how well you till the soil.
Scott Reed

When I found the potter's wheel, I felt it all
over like a wild duck in water.
George Ohr, *The Mad Potter of Biloxi*

There's no sense in arguing with them. Folks around
here are stubborn as they come.
Martha Foose

HUMAN SPIRIT

We most earnestly desire to become one not merely in community of
language and literature and traditions and country;
but… one also in feeling and heart.
LQC Lamar

I decline to accept the end of man. I believe man will not
merely endure — he will prevail.
William Faulkner, Nobel Prize address

Take a chance, will you? Just take some sort of chance!
Beth Henley, *Crimes of the Heart*

It's not enough to know what you're against.
Shelby Foote to John Carr

The togetherness… of Mississippi… is a togetherness born of the
struggle of man against river, man against conquering man, man
against plague, man against prejudice, man against a dead, deadly past,
and man against the questioning Cain, who is his worse self.
Hodding Carter, *Where Main Street Meets the River*

But how much better, in any case, to wonder than not to wonder, to
dance with astonishment and go spinning in praise, than
not to know enough to dance or praise at all.
Eudora Welty

The man who said it couldn't be done is usually
passed by the man who's doing it.
Paige Mitchell, *Wilderness of Monkeys*

The thing that got me was that John Whitelaw cared
so much about what he was doing.
Barry Hannah, *Airships*, "Midnight and I'm Not Famous Yet"

I am here and you will know that I am the best and will hear me. The
color of my skin or the kink of my hair or the spread of my mouth
has nothing to do with what you are listening to.
Leontyne Price

I prefer to leave standing up, like a well-mannered guest at a party.
Leontyne Price, on her retirement from opera

True tolerance cannot be legislated.
Frank Smith, congressman from Mississippi

Make Voyages! Attempt them! There's nothing else.
Tennessee Williams, *Camino Real*

It doesn't cost anything to be nice.
Boo Ferriss

Where there is no struggle, there is no strength.
Oprah Winfrey

If you want to accomplish the goals of your life,
you have to begin with the spirit.
Oprah Winfrey

If you come to fame not understanding who you
are, it will define who you are.
Oprah Winfrey

…his puny inexhaustible voice, still talking.
William Faulkner, Nobel Prize address

…a life's work in the agony and sweat of the human spirit… to create
out of the materials of the human spirit something
which did not exist before.
William Faulkner, Nobel Prize address

We should remember those times when the ideas of individuality of
excellence compounded of resourcefulness and independence and
uniqueness not only deserved a blue ribbon, but got one.
William Faulkner, address to American Academy of Arts and Letters

…The wit and wisdom… of any man who had watched human folly
yet still remained capable of believing in human aspirations.
William Faulkner

By artist I mean, of course, everyone who has tried to create something which was not here before him, with no other tools and material than the uncommercial one of the human spirit.

William Faulkner, National Book Award address

The human spirit obeys no physical laws.

William Faulkner, Athens Academy remarks

…the moment in 1492 when somebody thought 'This is it: the absolute edge of no return, to turn back now and make home or sail irrevocably on and either find land or plunge over the world's roaring rim.'

William Faulkner, *Intruder in the Dust*

Some things you must always be unable to bear. Some things you must never stop refusing to bear. Injustice and outrage and dishonor and shame.

William Faulkner, *Intruder in the Dust*

The only immortality we can be sure of is that part of ourselves we invest in others, the contribution we make to the totality of man, the knowledge we have shared, the truths we have found, the causes we have served, the lessons we have lived.

Wyatt Cooper, *Families*

Authority was something to be controverted, not conceded without contention.

Will Campbell

HUMILITY

We have strayed too far from the humble things that endure and given
short shrift to the rituals and traditions that give meaning
and continuity to our lives.
Sela Ward, *Homesick*

Any of us who needed humbling got it. Those who were already
humble realized that true humility has no limits.
Robert Khayat, *The Education of a Lifetime*

Maybe what I mean by truth is humility, and maybe what I think is
humility is really immitigable pride.
William Faulkner

William Winter is a rare politician: a humble man
with little to be humble about.
David Crews

Did we just get kicked out of a leper dance?
Neil White, *In the Sanctuary of Outcasts*

HUMOR

When Aunt Bama dies, either she or God has got to
leave Heaven, because both of 'em can't be boss.
William Faulkner

I taught Willie Morris algebra in high school. He always said he liked
me better than algebra, and I knew that to be the gospel truth.
Harriet DeCell Kuykendall

Indecision may or may not be my problem.
Jimmy Buffett

Shoot up here amongst us. One of us has got to have some relief.
Jerry Clower

I'm married to a nice man who's a dentist.
We have children with perfect teeth.
Richard Ford, *The Sportswriter*

I believe he's going to go in a tight end and come out a wide receiver.
Steve Holland, on prison time for Everette Dutschke who
was sentenced for sending ricin to President Obama

Jon Stewart: Is being secretary of the navy a good job?
Ray Mabus: It's a great job!
Jon Stewart: Why?
Ray Mabus: Because people salute me. They don't salute the
secretary of agriculture.
Jon Stewart, *The Daily Show*

I want you guys to gather in a round circle.
Coach Jake Gibbs to the Ole Miss baseball team

Making boring people seem interesting since 1982.
Motto of **Slim Smith**, *Columbus Dispatch* columnist

I spy a middle-aged woman waving her arms at the ticket
counter like a sprinklerhead gone awry.
Jonathan Miles, *Dear American Airlines*

Judge, please throw me in jail. That would be a vacation
after all the work and trouble folks have put on me.
Johnny Ray Strong, refusing to pay a fine

Ella Bounds: What you readin'?
Neil White: Self-help books.
Ella Bounds: They helpin'?
Neil White, *In the Sanctuary of Outcasts*

We will be offering continuous coverage of the
War in the Gulf, from time to time.
Jackson radio announcer

I faint every time I learn I'm about to have house guests.
Charlotte Capers

The Front Entrance Is In The Back.
Sign on front of Miss. State Auditor's Office in the 1990s

If you can't trust a trusty, who can you trust?
Ross Barnett

Oh, how I do love having birthday cake for breakfast! How I do!
Beth Henley, *Crimes of the Heart*

Here I am just practically on the brink of utter doom.
Beth Henley, *Crimes of the Heart*

You boys pair off. Pair off in threes.
Mississippi high school football coach

Faulkner's as popular as a dead skunk in a sleeping bag.
Oxford resident

After I shot him, I put the gun down on the piano bench, and then I
went out into the kitchen and made up a pitcher of lemonade.
Beth Henley, *Crimes of the Heart*

Old Granddaddy… told us not to cry anymore 'cause he was
gonna take us out to get banana splits for breakfast.
Beth Henley, *Crimes of the Heart*

Lenny: Just why did you take one little bite out of each piece
of candy in this box and then just put it back in?
Meg: Well, I was looking for the ones with nuts.
Beth Henley, *Crimes of the Heart*

You're just as perfectly sane as anyone walking
the streets of Hazlehurst, Mississippi.
Beth Henley, *Crimes of the Heart*

Lenny: My! Will you look at all those candles –
it's absolutely frightening.
Beth Henley, *Crimes of the Heart*, Lenny at her 30th birthday

Elain: You tried to choke Carnelle's poor father to death.
Delmount: I did it. But he was boring me to death.
Beth Henley, *Miss Firecracker*

Give him ten yards' head start, then shoot him like a dog.
Hodding Carter, jesting order to British troops who
had arrested one of his Yank correspondents

Who would want perfection without the intervening
contrast that makes perfection recognizable?
Hodding Carter, *Main Street*

It don't make no difference how you say it, just say it in a way that
makes sense. Did you ever meet anybody in your life who
didn't know what ain't means?
Dizzy Dean

Some people who don't say ain't, ain't eating.
Dizzy Dean

Where do folks get off criticizing my grammar? I only went to the
second grade, and if I'd gone to the third, I'd a passed my old man.
Dizzy Dean

If you cannot garden yourself, choose neighbors who can.
This is equally inspiring and less exhausting.
Charlotte Capers, *The Capers Papers*

The neighborhood had gathered, in various stages of
Sunday dress and undress, to admire the wreck.
Charlotte Capers, *The Capers Papers*

I think some of the evangelical signs from country roads should be
transferred to city streets, like 'Prepare to meet your God.'
Charlotte Capers, *Capers Papers*, after witnessing a car wreck in Jackson

I had two lovely children by an early and forgettable marriage.
Charlotte Capers, *The Capers Papers*, quoting a friend

Exaggeration is one of her splendid accomplishments.
Eudora Welty, on Charlotte Capers

…mobile homes… (that) had not moved in decades.
John Grisham, *The Firm*

You boys (FBI) have been watching and waiting for seven years...
Do you always move so fast?
John Grisham, *The Firm*

I grew up in a family whose concept of an adventure was not
confirming hotel reservations. In writing. Preferably twice.
Stuart Stevens, *Night Train to Turkistan*

My father announced that as far as these beautiful, unspoiled places
were concerned, he'd just as soon go back to when they
spoiled them a little more.
Stuart Stevens, *Night Train to Turkistan*

We were lost, but this was nothing new. Our state of orientation
continually oscillated between mildly confused and
hopelessly, no-idea-where-the-hell-we-were-lost.
Stuart Stevens, *Night Train to Turkistan*

The day started on a calamitous note.
Stuart Stevens, *Night Train to Turkistan*

The cookies had no taste whatsoever… I broke off a piece of the box
and chewed on it. While the textures were slightly different,
the taste was indistinguishable.
Stuart Stevens, *Night Train to Turkistan*

…ugly as a shotgunned butt of pork.
Barry Hannah, *Geronimo Rex*

It gives me a pleasant sense of the goodness of creation to think of the
brick and the glass and the aluminum being extracted from common
dirt — though no doubt it is less a religious sentiment than a financial
one, since I own a few shares of Alcoa.
Walker Percy, *The Moviegoer*

I subscribe to *Consumer Reports*, and as a consequence, I own a first-class
television set, an all-but-silent air conditioner, and a very
long-lasting deodorant. My armpits never stink.
Walker Percy, *The Moviegoer*

I have had the honor of serving upon this floor with the gentleman
from Ohio (Congressman Grosvenor) for a number of years, and his life
has been devoted to pouring oil on troubled waters.
Congressman "Private" John Allen

If the gentleman from Alabama expressly contradicted what I have
stated, he was in error and I am right.
Congressman "Private" John Allen

Congressman "Private" John Allen: I've talked with the
old boys and they say they have
nothing whatever against you, for you
did them less harm than any man
who fought on the other side.
Colonel George Peck: Having seen where John Allen lives, I
can never forgive myself for fighting
to keep it in the Union.
Congressman "Private" John Allen, when Colonel George Peck, a Yankee general
and friend of Allen, came to Vicksburg to deliver a speech. "Private" John
Allen invited him to a gathering of Confederate veterans.

Stella: They're Stanley's friends. They're a mixed lot.
Blanche: Heterogeneous-types?
Stella: Oh, yes. Yes, types is right!
Tennessee Williams, *A Streetcar Named Desire*

It was up to you to remember what you came for…
Eudora Welty, on going shopping as a little girl for her mother

Q: Governor, what do you think should be done with Quemoy and Matsu?
Governor Ross Barnett: I think I'll put 'em on the Game and Fish Commission.
Governor Ross Barnett, when asked about two disputed islands in the Pacific

This is Jim Saggus of A&P.
Governor Ross Barnett introducing Associated Press reporter Jim Saggus

You know how to fix it, don't you? Turn it off.
Barry Gossett, on malfunctioning electronic equipment

Federal Agent: Got any I.D.?
Suspect: About what?
Agent, holding up his own driver's license: Not idea, I.D.
Suspect, looking at the photo: That ain't me.

How could they make a wall out of China?
Seems like it would break mighty easy.
John Brandon Brewer's response when told about the Great Wall of China.

Stay fit and live long and prosper, but write your own obituary now, while you can, just in case.
Jill Connor Browne, *The Sweet Potato Queens Book of Love*

The court has viewed Woody Allen's movie, *Midnight in Paris*, read the book, *Requiem for a Nun*, and is thankful that the parties did not ask the court to compare *The Sound and the Fury* with *Sharknado*.
Opinion by **Judge Mike Mills** in *Faulkner v. Sony Pictures*

Hear ye, hear ye, hear ye. The United States District Court of the
Northern District of Mississippi is now open according to law. Judge
Glenn Davidson presiding... God save us.

CSO Ken Magness opening court. He should have said
"God save the United States and this honorable court."

The best thing since hairspray in the can.

Kathryn Stockett, *The Help*

So I drive into town for my first date in two years in a red 1941
Chevrolet four-on-the-floor with a John Deere
motor grader hooked behind me.

Kathryn Stockett, *The Help*

Aibileen can still tell a dirty joke that'll make you tinkle in your pants.

Kathryn Stockett, *The Help*

Tell him I said he better behave. Or I put him on my prayer list.

Kathryn Stockett, *The Help*

I intend to stay on her like hair on soap.

Kathryn Stockett, *The Help*

That was a wasted thought.

Eddie Rambo to friend who had made a weak, stupid comment

Oh Mama, leave Daddy alone. We don't want
to interrupt his perfect little world.

Jennifer Rambo

Manufactured in Detroit. Reassembled in Prentiss County.

Bumper sticker on pick-up truck in Prentiss County,
which was notorious for auto theft and chop shops

We always thought of Davy as just a member of the
family until Walt Disney discovered him.

Servetus Crockett, relative of Davy Crockett

Anyone who uses mascara knows you can fake stuff up.

Felder Rushing, on using artificial plants

If bullshit was music, that boy would be playing in a brass band.
Danny McKittrick

That was the summer Dill came to us… 'I'm Charles Baker Harris. I can read. You got anything needs reading, I can do it'… Dill was from Meridian, Mississippi.
Harper Lee, *To Kill a Mockingbird*

Count No Count
Nickname for Faulkner coined by Oxford residents

Never again will I be at the beck and call of every son-of-a-bitch who's got two cents to buy a stamp.
William Faulkner, on resigning as postmaster

'We not only want to honor this particular fellow Mississippian, we want him to honor us.'
An invitation to William Faulkner to speak to the Delta Council
'You can't beat that. To reverse a metaphor, that is a sword with not only two edges, but with both edges on the same side.'
William Faulkner

Hollywood is the only place you can get stabbed in the back while you're climbing a ladder.
William Faulkner to Shelby Foote

I'm a hard bloke to get along with.
William Faulkner to reporter

Chamber of Commerce race for Miss Sewage Disposal.
William Faulkner, mocking chamber of commerce hucksterism

I'll bet you could remove all those people who were there yesterday from the face of the earth, and nobody'd say anything.
William Faulkner, on a French fashion show

…the giveaway icebox — or — electric washer quiz programs (with questions like) what day of the month is the Fourth of July?
William Faulkner, letter to *New York Times*

Tell him he can go then. Tell him he had the wrong address...
Tell him we had a flood, even a freeze.
William Faulkner, *The Hamlet*, Prince of Hell on Flem Snopes

When Norman Mailer wrote that the white man feared the Negroes'
sexual potency, Faulkner replied, 'I have heard this idea expressed
several times during the last twenty years, though not before by a man.
The others were ladies, northern or middle western ladies, usually
around 40 or 45 years of age. I don't know what a
psychiatrist could find in this.'
William Faulkner, *The Independent*

The only thing memorable about Alabama is the
signs 'Jesus Saves' and 'Seven Killed Here'.
William Faulkner to Neil Thornton of UVA

Woman questioner: Mr. Faulkner, I understand that an
author always put himself in his books. Which character
are you in *Sanctuary*?
William Faulkner: Madam, I was the corncob.

I have absolutely no idea what I meant.
William Faulkner, on obscure passage in *The Sound and the Fury*

I don't like Jews — but I don't like Gentiles neither.
William Faulkner to Daniel Fuchs

I'd want to come back a buzzard. Nothing hates him or envies him or
needs him. He is never bothered or in danger, and he can eat anything.
William Faulkner, on reincarnation, *Paris Review*

Oh, those are secret agents without any secrets.
Battle Crews at age 10, upon discovering that U.S. Secret
Service agents are not James Bond-style secret agents

When I grow up, I'm going to be a fireman or a rocket scientist or a
dolphin trainer. Or, I don't know, maybe I'll just go to
the office every day like Daddy.
Lowrey Crews

Robert Khayat: Where do you keep your grits?
New England grocery store manager: Try international foods.

Willie Morris: Eudora, should we go down Paradise Lane?
Eudora Welty: Willie, I'm absolutely certain that we should.

Sign on a building: No loitering and no soliciting.
Eudora Welty's friend: Let's go in and loiter and solicit.
Eudora Welty: Let's do. I'll loiter. You solicit.

There are little fishes all over America clamoring to be born in Tupelo, Mississippi.
Congressman "Private" John Allen, advocating locating the National Fish Hatchery in Tupelo

Tupelo, Mississippi, is the center of the universe. You ask how I've ascertained this. Well, when I go out on the front porch of my home in Tupelo the horizon is equidistant on all sides. Why at high noon, the sun is directly overhead .
Congressman "Private" John Allen

The undertaker will let you down before I will.
Lee Abraham

It's a country-ass country club, and we're not big on rules and regulations.
Bill Luckett, on the Delta's Bayou Bend Country Club

Morgan's played God twice in the movies, and it's rubbed off on him some.
Bill Luckett, trying to make Morgan Freeman miss a golf putt

That's a long way to go just to eat.
William Faulkner, declining an invitation to dine with President Kennedy at the White House

I'm going to New Orleans to see that play by Tennessee Williams, *Fiddler on the Roof*, and I want to read it first.
Request to the librarian at the Eudora Welty Library in Jackson

Dunleith, the antebellum mansion that I always say makes Tara from *Gone with the Wind* look like a woodshed.

Greg Iles, *The Death Factory*

You can lead a horse to water, but you can't make him sing opera.

Richard Ford

I don't look in mirrors anymore. It's cheaper than surgery.

Richard Ford, *Let Me Be Frank with You*

There are two things I'd like to have from that reception… a picture of Aaron Henry kissing Jim Eastland… and a picture of Jim Eastland when he realized someone had a picture of Aaron kissing him.

Senator Ted Kennedy following a reception in Oxford at which state NAACP Chairman Aaron Henry kissed Jim Eastland

It's great to be among friends, even if they aren't your own.

Jack Reed

Coach Adolph Rupp: Butch, don't let the pressure of this game get to you.
Butch Lambert, SEC basketball referee: Coach, if I can call games between Baldwyn and Booneville High Schools, I can easily stand the pressure of a championship game between Kentucky and Vanderbilt.

Three hens, one rooster, and a duck.

George Ohr's description of his family; he was the duck

Mr. Ohr wishes to explain that the prefix Rev. to his name does not signify that he is a preacher. It only means that he is worthy of Reverence, because he does his work as well as he can, and Minds his own Business.

George Ohr, *The Mad Potter of Biloxi*

Old Diz knows the King's English. And not only that, I also know the Queen is English.

Dizzy Dean

HUNTING

...all three of us was still what we was — that old buck that had run...
because running was what he done the best and was proudest at, and
Eagle and the dogs that chased him... because that was the thing they
done the best and was proudest at; and me and Mister Ernest and Dan,
not because we wanted his meat... or his head to hang on a wall, but
because now we could go back and work hard for eleven months
making a crop, so we could have the right to come
back here next November.

William Faulkner, *Race At Morning*

...all three of us going back home now, peaceful and separate,
but still side by side, until next year, next time.

William Faulkner, *Race At Morning*

...a deed to ten acres of a defunct duck club in St. Bernard Parish,
the only relic of my father's many enthusiasms.

Walker Percy, *The Moviegoer*

He was a man of sixty and could neither read nor write, but he had all
the dignity of an African chief, and for half a century, he had been a
bear hunter, having killed or assisted in killing
over three thousand bears.

President Theodore Roosevelt, on Holt Collier

I am going on this hunt to kill a bear... When I hunt, I hunt. I
don't go for companionship — I go to get the game.

President Theodore Roosevelt, on hunting bear in Mississippi

My experience is that to try to combine a hunt and a picnic, generally
means a poor picnic, and always means a spoiled hunt.

President Theodore Roosevelt, on hunting in Mississippi

No hunter was equal in skill or courage to Holt Collier.

Minor Buchanan

Didn't do nothing much 'cept hunt.

Holt Collier

People here talk about firearms and hunting in the same way that urban liberals go on about nutrition and exercise.
Richard Grant, *Dispatches from Pluto*

I felt sad, upset, shaky, and proud all at the same time.
Richard Grant, *Dispatches from Pluto*, on his first kill

JUSTICE

But above all the courthouse: the center, the focus, the hub; sitting,
looming in the center of the county's circumference like a single cloud
in its ring of horizon, laying its vast shadow to the uttermost rim of
horizon; musing, brooding, symbolic, and ponderable, tall as cloud,
solid as rock, dominating all: protector of the weak, judicate and curb
of the passions and lusts, repository and guardian of
the aspirations and the hopes...
William Faulkner, *Requiem for a Nun*

It was not God's plan for your life for you to be in my courtroom
today. But you are here, and we must deal with it.
Judge Allen Pepper

Don't say anything that will get the judge off his script.
Defense attorney to his client

Be careful what you say. You don't want the judge to start thinking.
Defense attorney to his client

That was the most dramatic breakfast I've ever
eaten. That was better than TV.
Elderly woman to U.S. Marshals following the arrest
of a double murder suspect in Ripley, Mississippi

Justice could be very swift in his courtroom.
John Grisham, *A Time to Kill*

The two most precious words in the Afro-English language: not guilty.
John Grisham, *A Time to Kill*

The system reflects society… It's as fair as biased,
emotional humans can make it.
John Grisham, *A Time to Kill*

You can win the case, and if you do, justice will prevail.
But if you lose it, justice will also prevail.
John Grisham, *A Time to Kill*

They're going to judge you. And they'll probably judge you according to their thoughts, their feelings, their neuroses – along with the facts.
Paige Mitchell, *A Wilderness of Monkeys*

The testimony… now belonged to these men, the jury; to be consciously or subconsciously interpreted, misinterpreted, believed, disbelieved, and used finally to support or undermine a verdict.
Paige Mitchell, *A Wilderness of Monkeys*

You broke in. Now you break out.
Mississippi woman who grabbed the balls of a man who broke into her home, and then called the police to have him arrested

I've been on the bench for a long time. I thought I'd seen everything. But I was wrong.
U.S. District Judge Neal Biggers during sentencing of a father and daughter. The father was both the father and grandfather of his daughter's children

You'll find precious little justice in Mississippi's Justice Courts.
Bill Cole

Are you sure?
Court clerk's response when a Mississippi Circuit Judge announced his ruling

That man is going to have a long time to think about what he's done. I can't change how he thinks, but I can change where he thinks it.
U.S. District Judge Neal Biggers

Decisions in court are often based more on cold feet than conscience.
Al Moreton

It ain't really stealing if you do it in broad daylight.
Explanation given by a robbery suspect

From the moment the defendants discovered that Meredith was a Negro, they engaged in a carefully calculated campaign of delay, harassment, and masterly inactivity.
Judge John Minor Wisdom, 5th Circuit Court of Appeals, June 25, 1962, on admitting James Meredith to Ole Miss

I helped make a pretty damn good storm here; hurricane-size storm.
Steve Patterson in federal court describing his actions that led to prison time

Defense attorney: Do you really think my client can get a fair trial in this county?

Mississippi Sheriff: He will either get a fair trial or he'll get the kind of trial he deserves.

California Probation Officer: He got 129 months? Good God, did he kill someone?

Mississippi Probation Officer: No. Our judges just don't think much of someone who steals from an old person.

If the goddamn law won't take up for me, I'll take up for myself.
Larry Brown, *Father & Son*

I fully intended to contempt.
Andrews Marschalk, when fined for contempt of Court

For 40 years, our state judicial system allowed murderers to roam our land. Night riders, church burners, beaters, and killers deserve no protection from sure justice.
Dick Molpus, on the Neshoba County killers of three civil rights workers in 1964

I learned a long time ago from Martin King that peace is not necessarily the absence of turmoil, but peace is the presence of love and justice. And there ain't going to be no peace until love and justice prevail.
Aaron Henry

There he is. That's the man.
"Preacher" Mose Wright on witness stand in the Emmett Till Murder Trial pointing at defendant Roy Bryant

LAWYERS

But now the land and the time too are changing; what will follow will
be a matter of consolidation, of pettifogging and doubtless chicanery in
which I would be a babe in arms but in which you, trained in the
law, can hold your own...
William Faulkner, *The Unvanquished*

...we put business ahead of everything.
John Grisham, *The Firm*

Happy lawyers are productive lawyers.
John Grisham, *The Firm*

They knew much more than they could talk about.
John Grisham, *The Firm*

...big shot lawyers, eating furiously and importantly, powerfully.
John Grisham, *The Firm*

...we're nothing but hired guns.
John Grisham, *The Firm*

You ask a lot of questions, Mitch.
And you don't have enough answers.
John Grisham, *The Firm*

They were lawyers, trained to argue five sides of every issue.
John Grisham, *The Firm*

I love juries. I love to pick them, talk to them, sway them, manipulate
them, even buy them, but they're unpredictable.
John Grisham, *The Summons*

I would have bribed any judge for that ruling. I've done it before.
I'll happily do it again.
John Grisham, *The Summons*

Will Barrett was a man… who understood logic,
but never operated under it.
Paige Mitchell, *A Wilderness of Monkeys*

A million facts climbed over one another inside his head. But no doubts.
Paige Mitchell, *A Wilderness of Monkeys*

…the words hid much more than they revealed.
Paige Mitchell, *A Wilderness of Monkeys*

He's our client, so he's right, so you go find out why he's right.
Paige Mitchell, *A Wilderness of Monkeys*

Better a good CPA than a half-assed lawyer.
Walker Percy, *Lancelot*

To be a lawyer, you need a doctorate in fuzz – not divinity.
Al Moreton

Ross Barnett was not a brilliant lawyer. He was a brilliant jury
manipulator, but I don't think anybody ever accused
Ross of knowing much law.
Dean Robert Farley, Ole Miss Law School

Ole Patterson. He not only can make it rain, he can make it storm.
Tim Balducci, on Steve Patterson, undercover FBI recording

We spent a year trying to think as diabolically as the tobacco industry.
Dickie Scruggs

Like Saint George, I want to slay those tobacco dragons.
Mississippi Attorney General Mike Moore

I'm alone and outgunned, scared, and inexperienced, but I'm right.
John Grisham, *The Rainmaker*

We backslide into what lawyers do best - talking about other lawyers. -
John Grisham, *The Rainmaker*

LIES & LIARS

You are lying aloud.
Mary Hamilton, *Trials of the Earth*

A willful, obstinate, unsavory, obnoxious, pusillanimous,
pestilential, pernicious, and perversable liar.
Mississippi politician's description of an opponent at the Neshoba County Fair

Oh, shoot! It's that lawyer. I don't want to see him... Just tell him I died.
Beth Henley, *Crimes of the Heart*

'I enjoy research,' said Mitch. They nodded and
acknowledged this obvious lie.
John Grisham, *The Firm*

He would not lie, had no desire to lie.
John Grisham, *The Firm*, Mitch prior to lying to his wife

He said not to trust anyone at The Firm.
John Grisham, *The Firm*

I don't lie. I cheat and bribe, but I don't lie.
John Grisham, *The Summons*

The more intelligent we are, the more intelligent lies we tell ourselves.
Paige Mitchell, *Wilderness of Monkeys*

...real stuff, which is almost always lying.
Barry Hannah, *Geronimo Rex*

Did you know that some psychological study or other proves statistically
that the average human being tells between twenty-three and one
hundred and thirty-seven lies a day?
Ellen Douglas, *A Lifetime Burning*

The Lord... He can't tell no lie.
Larry Brown, *Dirty Work*

Blanche: You haven't said a word about my appearance.
Stella: You look just fine.
Blanche: God love you for a liar.
> **Tennessee Williams**, *A Streetcar Named Desire*

Blanche: You know I haven't put on one ounce in ten years?
> **Tennessee Williams**, *A Streetcar Named Desire*

Blanche: I know I fib a good deal. After all, a woman's charm is fifty percent illusion.
> **Tennessee Williams**, *A Streetcar Named Desire*

Stella: What are you laughing at, honey?
Blanche: Myself, myself for being such a liar!
> **Tennessee Williams**, *A Streetcar Named Desire*

Mitch: Lies, lies, inside and out, all lies.
Blanche: Never inside, I didn't lie in my heart…
> **Tennessee Williams**, *A Streetcar Named Desire*

I have to lie to her on a regular basis, which is in itself enjoyable, but a little degrading at the same time.
> **Kathryn Stockett**, *The Help*

Some things you just can't lie about.
> **Kathryn Stockett**, *The Help*

Can't lie to God.
> **Kathryn Stockett**, *The Help*

Sometimes, in order to tell the truth, a writer must lie a little.
> **Willie Morris**

Bilbo can make you believe him even when you know he's lying.
> **Greenwood resident** after a speech delivered by Theodore Bilbo

That man made me lie. He only asked me questions he already knew the answer to.
> **Witness** on the stand during questioning by Federal Prosecutor Charlie Spillers

Tonight, we're going to make the lie true.
Tennessee Williams, *Cat on a Hot Tin Roof*

I even had, in fact, a number of different voices... even if what I was
saying was a total lie and as distant from the
truth as Athens is from Nome.
Richard Ford, *The Sportswriter*

When it comes to the obituary, it is important not to lie outright.
Gayden Metcalfe, *Being Dead Is No Excuse*

As opposition researchers, we are admittedly attracted to lies.
Michael Rejebian, *We're With Nobody*

He said he was a liar by profession, and he made good money at it.
William Faulkner, *Mosquitos*

I do not believe there lives the Southern writer who can say without
lying that writing is fun to him. Perhaps we do not want it to be.
William Faulkner

We have become a nation of bragging, sentimental,
not-too-courageous liars.
William Faulkner, letter to Lambert Davis

Never be afraid to raise your voice for honesty and truth and
compassion, against injustice and lying and greed.
William Faulkner, address to University High School

I will never lie again. It's too much trouble. It's too much like trying to
prop a feather upright in a saucer of sand. There's never any end to it.
You never get any rest. You're never finished.
William Faulkner, *The Reivers*

If by going to Russia... I could free one Anna Karenina or Cherry
Orchard, I would do so. But to go there now...
would be not only a lie but a betrayal.
William Faulkner, letter to U.S. State Dept.

The only thing worse than a liar is a liar that's also a hypocrite.
Tennessee Williams

Most of the confidence which I appear to feel, especially when influenced by noon wine, is only a pretense.
Tennessee Williams

Antichrist, Beelzebub, deceiver, destructor, liar, seven heads and ten horns, oh Satan, the devil himself — that's the Carolyn McAdams I know.
Greenwood Police Chief describing the Mayor of Greenwood

…in our time liars and thieves and whores and adulterers wish also to be congratulated by the great public, if their confession is sufficiently psychological or strikes a sufficiently heartfelt and authentic note of sincerity.
Walker Percy, *The Moviegoer*

Albert had summoned all his courage and lied with the sincerity of Lucifer himself.
Greg Iles, *Natchez Burning*

Judge George Adams, who I was scared of as a young attorney, told me to get some cases in his court, noting that he would not cause me any problems. Well that turned out to be a lie.
Judge Mike Mills

We go on together living a lie
Because neither one of us
Wants to be the first to say goodbye.
Jim Weatherly, "Neither One of Us"

He'd perfected the art of lying while looking his victim right in the eye.
Bill Dunlap, *Short Mean Fiction*

Newgene Ledbetter was a full-blooded, registered, pedigreed liar.
Jerry Clower

It's amazing how lies grow.
John Grisham, *The Client*

LIFE

Better to come to Earth in New Jersey than not to come at all.
Richard Ford, *The Sportswriter*

A high station in life is earned by gallantry. Appalling
experiences are survived with grace.
Tennessee Williams

I started reading literature at seventeen or eighteen,
and I felt this extra beat to life.
Richard Ford

We are all sentenced to solitary confinement inside
our own skins for life.
Tennessee Williams

There's a lot to be said for doing what you're not supposed to do, and
the rewards of doing what you're supposed to do are more subtle and
take longer to become apparent, which maybe makes it less attractive.
But your life is the blueprint you make after the building is built.
Richard Ford

Human beings dream of life everlasting… But most of them
want it on Earth and not in heaven.
Tennessee Williams, *Cat on a Hot Tin Roof*

I thought a fabulous home and fast boats would make us a happy
family. But Neil and Maggie felt completely at home in a tiny room that
was designed for leprosy patients and now housed federal convicts.
Neil White, *In the Sanctuary of Outcasts*

Let's go sit out on the porch and watch the world go by.
Mrs. R.L. "Mama" Ray

Nobody seems to want me, or lend me a helping hand
My pocket book is empty and my heart is full of pain
I'm a thousand miles away from home, just waiting for a train.
Jimmie Rodgers, "Waiting for a Train"

Books, the books that I loved above all else to spend my time with, were the great tools for understanding one's life and the lives of other people.

Ellen Douglas, *Witnessing*

...all life requires of us, by George, is to find
one reason a day to go on.

Jonathan Miles, *Dear American Airlines*

Every place is different, but every place is the same,
because you carry yourself with you wherever you go.

Steve Yarbrough

At the age of twenty, I failed to grasp the difference between guilt,
which can almost always be atoned for, and
grief, which can only be borne.

Steve Yarbrough

The human race is just getting started... The cerebral cortex is only
a hundred thousand years old. It's still a baby, sucking teat and eating
Cheerios. We might get better, maybe even wise, if we can
last another thousand years.

Ellen Gilchrist, *A Dangerous Age*

I have been moving around all my life. Going to different schools, living
in different houses, shedding old roles, assuming new ones... I am a
human being, capable of mimicking anything I see or
remember or can imagine.

Ellen Gilchrist, *Falling Through Space*

These are my people, this is where I come from. We're givin' this life
everything we got and then some. It ain't always pretty, but it's real...

Rivers Rutherford, "These Are My People "

My characters generally embodied the attitude that life is always going
to be a damn nasty and probably baffling business, but
somebody has to go slogging through it.

Richard Ford, *The Sportswriter*

None of our lives is really ordinary; nothing humdrum
in our delights or our disasters.
Richard Ford, *The Sportswriter*

Once… I even dreamed of doing something great. But there is much to
be said for giving up such grand ambitions and living the
most ordinary life imaginable.
Walker Percy, *The Moviegoer*

I just hope we find a home up yonder where we can keep on
working. I don't want to stop working.
Theora Hamblett

Life has got to go on. No matter what happens,
you've got to keep on going.
Tennessee Williams, *A Streetcar Named Desire*

I wondered if there was some pattern or an order to things in your
life… or was everything just happening all the time, in a whirl
without anything to stop it or cause it.
Richard Ford, *Wildlife*

I try to take every conflict, every experience,
and learn from it. Life is never dull.
Oprah Winfrey

You should always know when you're shifting gears in life.
You should leave your era; it should never leave you.
Leontyne Price

Life is all memory, except for the one present moment that goes
by you so quickly you hardly catch it going.
Tennessee Williams

The art of living your life has a lot to do with getting over loss.
The less the past haunts you, the better.
Richard Ford

Never think you've seen the last of anything.
Eudora Welty

All experience is an enrichment rather than an impoverishment.
Eudora Welty, *One Writer's Beginnings*

For her life, any life, she had to believe, was
nothing but the continuity of its love.
Eudora Welty, *The Optimist's Daughter*

For there is hate as well as love, she supposed, in the coming
together and continuing of our lives.
Eudora Welty, *The Optimist's Daughter*

The fantasies of dying could be no stranger than the fantasies of living.
Survival is perhaps the strangest fantasy of them all.
Eudora Welty, *The Optimist's Daughter*

Human life is fiction's only theme.
Eudora Welty, *On Writing*

The difficulty that accompanies you is less like the dark
than a trusted lantern to see your way by.
Eudora Welty

Every day is not perfect.
Brett Favre

You know, I've had my ups and downs.
Brett Favre

Men can starve from a lack of self-realization as much as
they can from a lack of bread.
Richard Wright

Everything takes me longer than I expect. It's a sad truth about life.
Donna Tartt

The more you learn, the more complicated it gets.
Morgan Freeman

The meaning of life, for every organism on the planet, including us, is to procreate and die. That's it. And you may as well enjoy the rest of it.
Morgan Freeman

James Lewis Carter "T-Model" Ford had made it just past his ninety-second birthday on a staple diet of fried chicken and Jack Daniels. The cause of death was having lived a long, full life.
Richard Grant, *Dispatches from Pluto*

There are some things, some of the hard facts of life, that you don't forget, no matter how old you are.
William Faulkner, *The Reivers*

...between grief and nothing, I will take grief.
William Faulkner, letter to Joan Williams

...it is never the thing that you did that you regret when it's too late, but the things you didn't do, didn't commit, didn't have.
William Faulkner, letter to Joan Williams

You ran from your heart and your body back into your mind, which is dead matter, nothing, since only the heart, the body, the nerves, are capable of feeling fire, anguish, passion, exultation, happiness, hope.
William Faulkner, letter to Joan Williams

...peace is only a condition in retrospect, when the subconscious has got rid of the gnats and the tacks and the broken glass in experience and has left only the peaceful pleasant things — that was peace. Maybe peace is not is, but was.
William Faulkner, to UVA English class (1957)

...the tragedy of life is it must be premature, inconclusive, and inconcludable, in order to be life; it must before itself, in advance of itself, to have been at all.
William Faulkner, *The Town*

The right track is the one that leads to life, to the sunlight. One cannot unceasingly suffer from the cold.
William Faulkner, on Albert Camus, *Transatlantic Review*, 1961

...he spent that life searching himself and demanding of himself
answers which only God could know.
William Faulkner, on Albert Camus

Romantic vision can also lead one away from certain very hard, ugly
truths about life that are important to know.
Donna Tartt

Our lives are trial and error, joy and sorrow, work and rest,
some peace and some turmoil...
Wyatt Cooper, *Families*

The fashion these days is for change and the rush for change... the pace
so accelerated that the less venturesome among us can get
quite dizzy even standing still and looking on.
Wyatt Cooper, *Families*

...loss is the key in which much of life is played.
Stuart Stevens, *The Last Season*

After a year in therapy, my psychiatrist said to
me, 'Maybe life isn't for everyone.'
Larry Brown, *Big Bad Love*

Some people want to be bank presidents.
Other people want to rob banks.
Richard Ford

You're only good if you can do bad and decide not to.
Richard Ford, *Canada*

Your life doesn't mean what you have or what you get.
It's what you're willing to give up.
Richard Ford, *Wildlife*

In my view, all teachers should be required to stop teaching at age
thirty-two and not allowed to resume until they're sixty-five, so that they
can live their lives, not teach them away — live lives full of ambiguity
and transience and regret and wonder.
Richard Ford

I'm trying to cause people to be interested in the particulars of their lives because I think that's one thing literature can do for us. It can say to us: pay attention. Pay closer attention. Pay stricter attention to what you say to your son.

Richard Ford

Things happen when people are not where they belong, and the world moves forward and back by that principle.

Richard Ford, *Canada*

But to anyone reasonable, my life will seem more or less normal under the microscope, full of contingencies and incongruities none of us escapes...

Richard Ford, *Independence Day*

In their faces — plenty of them were handsome, but ruined — I've seen the remnants of who they almost succeeded in being but failed to be, before becoming themselves.

Richard Ford, *Canada*

...I am unsure now if life has not suddenly passed me like a big rumbling semi and left me flattened here by the road.

Richard Ford, *The Sportswriter*

I thought that the difference between a successful life and an unsuccessful one... was how well you were able to put things like this out of your mind and not be bothered by them.

Richard Ford, *Rock Springs*

Meeting a girl, falling in love, marrying her, moving to Connecticut, buying a fucking house, starting a life with her and thinking you really knew anything about her — the last part was a complete fiction, which made all the rest a joke.

Richard Ford, *A Multitude of Sins*

It's hard to go through life without killing someone.

Richard Ford, *Canada*

There's no right way to plan a life and no right way
to live one — only plenty of wrong ways.
Richard Ford, *Let Me Be Frank with You*

...for your life to be worth anything, you must sooner or later face the
possibility of terrible, searing regret. Though you must also
manage to avoid it, or your life will be ruined.
Richard Ford, *The Sportswriter*

The things you'll never do don't get decided at the end of life, but
somewhere in the long, gray middle, where you can't see
the dim light at either end.
Richard Ford, *The Lay of the Land*

If there's another thing that sportswriting teaches you, it is that there
are no transcendent themes in life.
Richard Ford, *The Sportswriter*

...nothing's worth doing unless it has the
potential to fuck up your whole life.
Richard Ford, *Independence Day*

Life is full of surprises, a wise man said, and would not be
worth having if it were not.
Richard Ford, *The Lay of the Land*

When you're young, your opponent is the future; but when you're not
young, your opponent's the past and everything you've done in it and
the problem of getting away from it.
Richard Ford, *Independence Day*

...our ongoing ignorance makes so much of life possible.
Richard Ford, *The Lay of the Land*

Very early on, you come to the realization that nothing
will ever take you away from yourself.
Richard Ford, *The Sportswriter*

What I know is you have a better chance in life — of surviving
it — if you tolerate loss well.
Richard Ford, *Canada*

That jail existed for the opposite reason from why your home existed.
Richard Ford, *Canada*

When everything is at risk, good judgment, not haste, makes the difference between life and death. Panic is the enemy.
Greg Iles

You are healthy, or you are sick. You are faithful to your wife, or you aren't. You are alive, or you are dead.
Greg Iles

Man is the universe becoming conscious of itself.
Greg Iles, *The Footprints of God*

Man plans; God laughs.
Greg Iles, *Natchez Burning*

There it was, the choice I'd confronted so often in life: the path of least resistance, or the walk over hot coals.
Greg Iles, *The Death Factory*

Sometimes it's about playing a poor hand well.
Donna Tartt, *The Goldfinch*

None of us ever find enough kindness in the world, do we?
Donna Tartt, *The Goldfinch*

Isn't everything worthwhile a gamble? Can't good come around sometimes through some strange back doors?
Donna Tartt, *The Goldfinch*

You can look at a picture for a week and never think of it again. You can also look at a picture for a second and think of it all your life.
Donna Tartt, *The Goldfinch*

…it all ends badly for all of us, even the happiest of us, and that we lose everything that matters in the end — and yet to know as well, despite all this, as cruelly as the game is stacked, that it's possible to play it with a kind of joy.
Donna Tartt, *The Goldfinch*

It's not about outward appearances, but inward significance.
Donna Tartt, *The Goldfinch*

Never do what you can't undo.
Donna Tartt, *The Goldfinch*

Any action, in the fullness of time, sinks to nothingness.
Donna Tartt, *The Secret History*

We think we have many desires, but in fact we have
only one... To live forever.
Donna Tartt, *The Secret History*

...stepping from the world of warmth and people and conversation
overheard, I felt the old familiar cold twist through my bones again, and
then it was all forgotten, the warmth, the lights; I had never
been warm in my life, ever.
Donna Tartt, *The Secret History*

It is dangerous to ignore the existence of the irrational.
Donna Tartt, *The Secret History*

Where there is chance of gain, there is also chance of loss. Whenever
one courts great happiness, one also risks malaise.
Walker Percy, *The Moviegoer*

It is not a bad thing to settle for the Little Way, not the big search for
the big happiness, but the sad little happiness of drinks and kisses, a
good little car, and a warm, deep thigh.
Walker Percy, *The Moviegoer*

Hatred strikes me as one of the few signs of life remaining in the world.
This is another thing about the world which is upside down: all the
friendly and likable people seem dead to me; only the haters seem alive.
Walker Percy, *The Moviergoer*

Whoever you are, be that person with all your might.
Barry Hannah

You need to see a bit of hell now and then. That, and great joy.
Barry Hannah

Adversity and success both contribute largely to making you what you
are. If you don't experience either one of those, you're
being deprived of something.
Shelby Foote

I abhor the idea of a perfect world. It would bore me to tears.
Shelby Foote

There is no surer sign of success in life than wearing
shorts during business hours.
Jim Dees

Over the generations of my family… there have been thieves,
adulterers, sociopaths, killers, racists, liars, and folks suffering from
panic attacks and real bad tempers, though to the best of my knowledge
we've never had a barn burner or a preacher.
Dean Faulkner Wells, *Every Day by the Sun*

It no longer seemed important to prove anything. I had found
something outside myself that gave meaning to my life.
Anne Moody, *Coming of Age in Mississippi*

We drank too much, smoked too much, were abusive to ourselves, to
each other. We were bewildered. There is a great darkness
bearing down on our lives, and no one acknowledges it.
Jesmyn Ward, *Men We Reaped*

Life is a hurricane.
Jesmyn Ward, *Men We Reaped*

Grief scabs over like scars and pulls into new, painful configurations
as it knits. It hurts in new ways. We are never free from grief. We are
never free from the feeling that we have failed. We are never free from
self-loathing. We are never free from the feeling that something
is wrong with us, not with the world that made this mess.
Jesmyn Ward, *Men we Reaped*

…this is how my brother and I understood what it meant to be a woman; working, dour, full of worry. What it meant to be a man: resentful, angry, wanting life to be everything but what it was.

Jesmyn Ward, *Men We Reaped*

"You fellows," I said, shaking my finger and raising an eyebrow, "have got to get serious about what you are doing or you will never succeed in the practice of law." I paused for dramatic effect. "Or elsewhere."

Mary Ann Connell, *An Unforeseen Life*, to Mike Mills,
Ronnie Musgrove, Roger Wicker, and John Grisham,

Life is much simpler ignoring reviews and the nasty people who write them. Critics should find meaningful work.

John Grisham

I had never been in a law enforcement facility
sober and of my own free will.

Jim Dees, *The Statue & the Fury*

Yeah, that much whip crème is definitely not good for you.

Jim Dees, *The Statue & the Fury*, on nakedness, whip crème, and
lewd acts at 2LiveCrew performance in Oxford

The first rule of holes is, when you find yourself in one, quit digging.

State Senator Hob Bryan

LOVE

The human race. You have to love it and wish it well and not preach or think you have any reason to think you are better than anyone else.
Ellen Gilchrist, *Acts of God*

Saw what I liked and liked what I saw
And my heart went along for the ride
Uh,oh, I'm falling in love again.
Jimmie Rodgers, "I'm Falling in Love Again"

To translate a literary work is to make love to a woman who will always be in love with someone else.
Jonathan Miles, *Dear American Airlines*

I don't believe you ever stop loving anyone you ever really loved… You can forget a lot of things in life, but not that honey to end all honeys.
Ellen Gilchrist, *A Dangerous Age*

The way you look, the way you laugh, the way you love with all you have, there ain't nothing 'bout you that don't do something for me.
Rivers Rutherford, "Ain't Nothing 'bout You"

Why should I be lonesome, when nobody is lonesome for me?
Jimmie Rodgers

Stand by your man. Give him two arms to cling to and something warm to come to when nights are cold and lonely.
Tammy Wynette

We have got rid of love at last…
William Faulkner, *Wild Palms*

…we are the two in all the world who can love each other without having to.
William Faulkner, *The Town*

…He loved the old few simple things… a little of music, a hearth, any child, a God, a heaven which a man may avail himself a little of at any time without having to wait to die, a little earth for his own sweat to fall on among his own green shoots and plants.

William Faulkner, *Intruder in the Dust*

The American really loves nothing but his automobile: not his wife, his child, nor his country, nor even his bank account first…Because the automobile has become our national sex symbol.

William Faulkner, *Intruder in the Dust*

Take the maestros advice and never, never, never fall in love.

William Faulkner, letter to Joan Williams

Why can't he understand we love him?
He doesn't understand a lot of things.

Paige Mitchell, *Wilderness of Monkeys*

They kissed… the kind they had enjoyed as teenagers when kissing was fun and mysterious and the ultimate.

John Grisham, *The Firm*

…you love everything and hate everything at the same time.

Barry Hannah, *Geronimo Rex*

All I say is bless God for the man-woman relationship.

Barry Hannah, *Nightwatchmen*

Will you tell me why I can only love in pieces? I can never get my head, my heart, and my body into it all together.

Barry Hannah, *Nightwatchmen*

Love the loss, as well as the gain.

Barry Hannah, *Airships*, "Midnight and I'm not Famous Yet"

You must let yourself be loved, and you must love, parts of you that never loved must open and love. You must announce yourself in all particulars, so you can have yourself.

Barry Hannah

I love you to a certain extent.
Thomas Harris, *Black Sunday*

I drew it in ecstasy.
Walter Anderson, *Horn Island Logs*

He fell in love at first sight and at a distance of two thousand feet.
Walker Percy, *The Last Gentleman*

What do you love? What do you live by?
Walker Percy, *The Moviegoer*

...love: it is an absolute and therefore beyond all categories.
Walker Percy, *Lancelot*

I discovered the secret of love. It is hate, or
rather the possibility of hate.
Walker Percy, *Lancelot*

Make love and not war? I'll take war rather
than what this age calls love.
Walker Percy, *Lancelot*

I live the life I love, and I love the life I live.
Willie Dixon, "I Love the Life I Live"

It could be a spoonful of coffee. It could be a spoonful of tea. But one
little spoonful of your precious love is good enough for me.
Willie Dixon, "Spoonful"

...the deep-grained habit of love.
Eudora Welty

The habit of love cuts through confusion and stumbles or
contrives its way out of difficulty.
Eudora Welty, Essay, "Is Phoenix Jackson's Grandson Really Dead?"

Living with someone you love can be lonelier than living entirely
alone — if the one that y'love doesn't love you.
Tennessee Williams, *Cat on a Hot Tin Roof*

I believe that every single event in life is an
opportunity to choose love over fear.
Oprah Winfrey

Hell is yourself, and the only redemption is when a person puts himself
aside to feel deeply for another person.
Tennessee Williams

The strongest influences in my life and my work are always whomever
I love. Whomever I love and am with most of the time, or whomever I
remember most vividly. I think that's true of everyone, don't you?
Tennessee Williams

Oh, you weak, beautiful people who give up with such grace. What you
need is someone to take hold of you — gently, with
love, and hand your life back to you.
Tennessee Williams

I think once you love somebody, you love somebody; that's just how it is.
Richard Ford

Love and despair go hand in hand.
Barry Hannah

Randomness I love. And I still love just a holler right in the
middle of an ongoing narrative. Pain or joy, ecstasy.
Barry Hannah

Nobody loves me but my mother, and she could be jivin' too.
B.B. King

A line can be straight like a street, but the human heart, oh no, it's
curved like a road through mountains.
Tennessee Williams

There is no urge to touch, to kiss, to embrace. But I do it just the same.
It is our last charm. Love isn't a thing, after all, but an
endless series of single acts.
Richard Ford, *Let Me Be Frank with You*

The saved moment is the true art of love.
Richard Ford, *The Sportswriter*

Strength lies in the qualities of compassion,
tolerance, understanding, and love.
Governor William Winter

Stay away from the ones you love too much.
Those are those ones who will kill you.
Donna Tartt, *The Goldfinch*

…how can I see so clearly that everything I love or care about is
illusion, and yet — for me, anyway — all that's worth
living for lies in that charm?
Donna Tartt, *The Goldfinch*

As long as I am acting out of love,
I feel I am doing the best I know how.
Donna Tartt, *The Goldfinch*

I add my own love to the history of people who have loved beautiful
things, and looked out for them, and pulled them from the fire, and
sought them when they were lost, and tried to preserve them and save
them while passing them along literally from hand to hand, singing out
brilliantly from the wreck of time to the next
generation of lover and the next.
Donna Tartt, *The Goldfinch*

If a painting really works down in your heart and changes the way you
see and think and feel, you don't think, 'Oh I love this painting because
it speaks to mankind'. That's not the reason anyone loves a piece of art.
It's a secret whisper from an alleyway. Psst, you. Hey, kid. Yes,
you. An individual heart shock.
Donna Tartt, *The Goldfinch*

I had grown up in that house; I couldn't have loved it more, couldn't have been more familiar with the creak of the swing... The very colors of the place had seeped into my blood.

Donna Tartt, *The Goldfinch*

Love doesn't conquer everything. And whoever thinks it does is a fool.

Donna Tartt, *The Secret History*

For every moment I've spent hurting
There was a moment spent loving you.

Jim Weatherly, "Best Thing That Ever Happened to Me"

When you're ready to come home
I'll still love you.

Jim Weatherly, "I'll Still Love You"

For love gonna board
The midnight train to Georgia.

Jim Weatherly, "Midnight Train to Georgia"

There is great pain in all love, but we don't care, it's worth it.

Lewis Nordan, *Music of the Swamp*

We love each other fiercely, while we live and after we die.

Jesmyn Ward, *Men We Reaped*

I think my love for books sprang from my need to escape the world I was born into, to slide into another where words were straightforward and honest, where there was clearly delineated good and evil, where I found girls who were strong and smart and creative and foolish enough to fight dragons...

Jesmyn Ward, *Men We Reaped*

I fell in love with Medgar before I fell in love with Myrlie.

Walter Williams, on his admiration for Medgar Evers long before he fell in love with and married Medgar's widow

MARRIAGE

Apparently man can be cured of drugs, drink, gambling, biting his nails, and picking his nose, but not of marrying.
William Faulkner

One thing I know is that it is a bad idea to marry someone who had bad parents. If they hated their mother, if they were hated by their mother or father, your marriage will pay for it in ways both obvious and subtle.
Ellen Gilchrist

Blanche: You can get out.
Stella: I'm not in anything I want to get out of.
Tennessee Williams, *A Streetcar Named Desire*

The closest I ever came to getting married was just before I started singing. In fact, my first record saved my neck.
Elvis Presley

When I get married, it'll be no secret.
Elvis Presley

Married life requires shared mystery even when all the facts are known.
Richard Ford

Writing is the only thing I've done with persistence, except for being married.
Richard Ford

I've been married twice. Most women would rather not be married to a traveling blues singer.
B.B. King

...a married, invincible bachelor without destination, but only motion.
William Faulkner, *Essay on Mississippi*

What could a marriage come to which was founded on the vanity of a weak man?
William Faulkner

The only life after death any human being will ever know is staying in a marriage or a partnership after it's over. And that's not
life — it's living death.
Greg Iles, *True Evil*

…the entire conception of knowing another person — of trust, of closeness, of marriage itself — was still completely out of date, defunct, was something typifying another era, now unfortunately gone.
Richard Ford, *A Multitude of Sins*

How could homosexuals possible screw up the sanctity
of marriage any worse than heterosexuals?
John Grisham, *The Appeal*

A battered wife is a married woman until she gets a divorce.
Or until she kills the bastard.
John Grisham, *The Rainmaker*

MEN

Poor Man. Poor Mankind
William Faulkner, *Light in August*

...his whole native land, his home — the dirt, the earth which has bred his bones and those of his fathers for six generations and was still shaping him into not just a man but a specific man... with specific passions and hopes, and convictions and ways of thinking...
William Faulkner, *Intruder in the Dust*

He is entirely self-possessed with a manner easy, courteous, speculative, and deadly.
Life **Magazine** description of William Faulkner

Albert Einstein was one of the wisest of men and one of the gentlest of men. Who can replace him in either, let alone in both?
William Faulkner, telegram to Saxe Commins

(Men) were capable of anything, any height or depth.
William Faulkner, *Go Down, Moses*

The Square: the edifices created and ordained for trade and government and judgment and incarceration where strove and battled the passions of men.
William Faulkner, *Intruder in the Dust*

Meg: You're your own woman. Invite some people over. Have some parties. Go out with strange men.
Lenny: I don't know any strange men.
Beth Henley, *Crimes of the Heart*

I'd done as poor a job of making a bad man as I had of making a good one.
Shelby Foote, *Shiloh*

Harley saw the movie just three times, being habitually a moderate man when it came to entertaining himself.
Barry Hannah, *Geronimo Rex*

A man who moved as if animal secrets were known to him.
Barry Hannah, *The Tennis Handsome*

He had to know everything before he could do anything.
Walker Percy, *The Last Gentleman*

Lucky is the man who does not secretly believe
that every possibility is open to him.
Walker Percy, *The Last Gentleman*

Both a scientific and superstitious turn of mind.
Walker Percy, *The Last Gentleman*

Don't you think a thirty-year-old man ought
to know what he wants to do with his life?
Walker Percy, *The Moviegoer*

He understands everything out there and everything
out there is something to be understood.
Walker Percy, *The Moviegoer*

Men… who would as soon do one thing as another as long as they can
go fishing, hunting, drink a bit, horse around, watch the
Dolphins and Jack Nicklaus on TV.
Walker Percy, *Lancelot*

Physically, he was the connoisseur's connoisseur. He was a giant panda,
Santa Claus, and the Jolly Green Giant rolled into one. On him, a lean
and slender physique would have looked like very bad casting.
Craig Claiborne, on James Beard

Crisco… meaning something you can't dress up no matter how hard
you try. We start call his daddy Crisco cause you can't
fancy up a man done run off with his family. Plus
he the greasiest no-count you ever known.
Kathryn Stockett, *The Help*

Willie Morris… the magic and the mystery and the misery in the man.
Larry L. King,

Here came this baby-faced rebel from Deep East Jesus.
Larry L King, *In Search of Willie Morris*

I've got another man I'm waiting on. And it's not Santy Claus,
and it's not the Baby Jesus. It's Mister Johnny Foote, Jr.
Kathryn Stockett, *The Help*

Men don't understand much… It's not their long suit. They
don't wake up crying either. Women take care of that.
Richard Ford, *Wildlife*

Men do not discuss with their wives (or mothers)
the business that is their own.
Tom Franklin, *Crooked Letter, Crooked Letter*

Larry's vehicle must be the most cared-for in the county,
a patient with its own full-time doctor.
Tom Franklin, *Crooked Letter, Crooked Letter*

A man in his forties, slammed with his past,
the kudzu moving faster than he was.
Tom Franklin, *Crooked Letter, Crooked Letter*

I'm kind of a distractible guy.
Richard Ford

Men are a strange breed.
Richard Ford, *Let Me Be Frank with You*

Beware a man with manners.
Eudora Welty

In the end, it takes phenomenal neatness of housekeeping to
put it through the heads of men that they are swine.
Eudora Welty, *The Collected Stories*

…our mothers: why they — angels, goddesses — had to die? while our
awful fathers thrived and boozed and sprawled and muddled
on and continued to stumble about and wreak havoc in
seemingly indefatigable health?
Donna Tartt, *The Goldfinch*

Growing up, I was taught that a man has to defend his family.
When the wolf is trying to get in, you gotta stand in the doorway.
B.B. King

A man's biggest enemy is his mouth.
Greg Iles, *Natchez Burning*

Did the fact that Martin Luther King diddled all those women change
what he did for his people? Or Franklin Roosevelt? General
Eisenhower? Not one whit. Men are men, and gods are for storybooks.
And if you've read your Edith Hamilton or Jane Harrison — or the
Old Testament for that matter — you'll know that gods
acted like men most of the time, or worse.
Greg Iles, *Natchez Burning*

One resolute man can sometimes accomplish remarkable
things against overwhelming odds.
Greg Iles, *Natchez Burning*

Nothing frightens me more than the faith in my daughter's eyes. How
many men deserve that kind of trust? One by one, the mentors I've
most admired eventually revealed chinks in their armor, cracks in their
facades, and tired feet of clay — or worse.
Greg Iles, *Natchez Burning*

Men fantasize about wanton women, but when
they meet one, they're paralyzed by fear.
Greg Iles, *Mortal Fear*

A gentleman accepts the responsibility of his actions and bears the bur-
den of their consequences, even when he did not himself
instigate them, but only acquiesced to them, didn't
say no, though he knew he should have.
William Faulkner

In this world, goodness is destined to be defeated. But a man
must go down fighting. That is the victory. To do
anything less is to be less than a man.
Walker Percy, *The Moviegoer*

...we hear a great many flattering things nowadays about your great common man — you know, it has already been revealing to me that he is perfectly content so to be called, because that is exactly what he is: the common man, and when I say common, I mean common as hell.

Walker Percy, *The Moviegoer*

...Fran was left in the dark with a single, over-arching emotion she would come to know time and again in her encounters with men: a deep and abiding disappointment.

Bill Dunlap, *Short Mean Fiction*

MISSISSIPPI

I am worn out and antagonistic to the idea that
we have to be fiftieth in everything.
George McLean

Loving all of it even while he had to hate some of it, because he knows
now that you don't love because; you love despite; not for
the virtues, but despite the faults.
William Faulkner, *On Mississippi*

Whole state of Missisippi ain't em there. Ain't no such of a place. Cross
over the Alabama line in the middle of the night, road don't change,
woods don't change, dirt don't change, night don't change. Ain't no
such of a thing, Mississippi. It's all just in your imagination.
Jack Butler, *Jujitsu for Christ*

We can't look to Washington and Jackson for help.
We have to do the job ourselves.
George McLean

The north was where he lived and worked, but it wasn't home.
Home was where Momma was, in Mississippi.
John Grisham, *A Time to Kill*

The first time I saw the Mississippi River, I was
trying to get up out of it.
B.B. King, on the Flood of 1927

I wanted to get out of Mississippi in the worst way.
Muddy Waters

We had to make our own fun back then in a little town.
But that was no problem with Willie (Morris) among us.
Honest Ed Upton

I learned more about the town's past here (Glendale Cemetery), the
migrations, the epidemics, the old forgotten tragedies, than
I ever could have learned in the library.
Willie Morris

We knew where our ancestors were buried; we took
care of their graves and we kept alive their stories.
Wyatt Cooper, *Families*

Mississippi — that's the worst state in the Union.
Robert Frost to Willie Morris

Everybody from Mississippi, bow your heads.
H.L. Mencken

James Meredith was a character so colorful and complex,
he could only have sprung from the rich soil of Mississippi.
William Doyle, *An American Insurrection*

The closed society of Mississippi comes as near to approximating a
police state as anything we have seen in America.
James Silver, *The Closed Society*

The President (Kennedy) issued the order for the U.S. Army to launch a
military invasion of Northern Mississippi to restore law and order.
William Doyle, *An American Insurrection*

Stand Fast, Mississippi!
Colonel Jefferson Davis to troops in the Mexican War, Battle of Buena Vista

Conversations in Mississippi have a smack of manslaughter about them.
William Howard Russell, *Times of London* correspondent

Northerners, provincials that they are, regard the South as one large
Mississippi. Southerners, with their eye for distinction,
place Mississippi in a class by itself.
V.O. Key, Jr.

It ain't but one thing I done wrong; I stayed in
Mississippi just a day too long.
Bob Dylan, Mississippi

M i crooked letter crooked letter i crooked letter
crooked letter i humpback humpback i.
Children's chant to spell Mississippi

Growing up, my goal was always to leave Mississippi.
Morgan Freeman, who returned to Mississippi after a successful acting career

I'm going to Mississippi.
Barack Obama, announcing that he would
show up for the first Presidential debate in 2008

One day we will not have to hang our heads in shame or hold our
breath when the name Mississippi is mentioned, fearing
the worst. But, instead, we will be anticipating the best.
Medgar Evers

As you can see, I do not plan to leave (Mississippi). I am anchoring
myself here for better or for worse. I hope for better, but if
worse comes, I'll be in the middle of it.
Medgar Evers

Where the Southern crosses the Dog — Moorhead, Mississippi.
Song lyric from the early 1900s, also a password used
by American soldiers during WWI

Mississippi is the Ireland of America. It's a green place where literature
and music are valued more than acquiring wealth. Drinking and
fighting are accepted and often respected social endeavors, and
defending one's honor is still considered worthy, if not mandatory.
Stuart Stevens, *The Daily Beast*, April 30, 2013

I always wanted to go to Africa. Well, I don't.
Mississippi's wild enough for me.
Larry Brown, *Father and Son*

I flew across the country recently and fulfilled one of my lifelong
dreams. I took a piss over the state of Mississippi.
Johnny Carson on *The Tonight Show*

I'm a native Mississippian, even though I was born in New York.
Comment by new resident

Spent a summer in your state. Got chased by a snake, dated a girl from Pascagoula whose brothers stomped me, and got terribly sunburned. Other than that, had a great time. Yours, Mike Royko

Note by Mike Royko, columnist and author who served in the Air Force at Keesler AFB

Wide open and wicked.

Clarion Ledger description of the Mississippi Gulf Coast

The Mafia has done a whole lot less damage to Mississippi than the Hedermans.

Biloxi Mayor Jerry O'Keefe after a *Clarion Ledger* story about Mafia influence on the Gulf Coast described the Mississippi Gulf Coast as "wide open and wicked."

More than anything else, I want the folks back home to think right of me.

Elvis Presley

They didn't give you too much schooling, because just as soon as you was big enough, you get to working in the fields.

Muddy Waters

We think as our land thinks.

Mississippi WPA Guide

I come from a people who put their family above all else, for better or worse.

Sela Ward

Mississippi is a place where great literature blossomed in a field of vast illiteracy.

Curtis Wilkie

Carroll County, a patch of worn-out Mississippi farmland heartbreaking in its meanness.

Curtis Wilkie, *George* Magazine

Everybody knows about Mississippi, Godddamn!

Nina Simone

Mississippi is the best-kept secret in America. Nowhere else is so poorly understood by outsiders, so unfairly maligned, so surreal and peculiar, so charming and maddening.
Richard Grant, *Dispatches from Pluto*

Mississippians have a kind of genius for charging after phantoms and lost causes.
Richard Grant, *Dispatches from Pluto*

Mississippi gives every appearance of being a redneck disaster zone.
Richard Grant, *Dispatches from Pluto*

There's America, there's the South, then there's Mississippi.
President Lyndon Johnson

It's Mississippi, everyone is going to assume we're armed to the teeth.
Richard Grant, *Dispatches from Pluto*

People here talk about firearms and hunting in the same way that urban liberals go on about nutrition and exercise.
Richard Grant, *Dispatches from Pluto*

I can live anywhere I want, and this is where I want to live.
Morgan Freeman, on Mississippi

I have a dream that one day even the state of Mississippi, a state sweltering with the heat of injustice, sweltering with the heat of oppression, will be transformed into an oasis of freedom and justice.
Martin Luther King Jr.

Let freedom ring from every hill and molehill of Mississippi.
Martin Luther King Jr.

I, too, like my town, my land, my people, my life, am unhappy away from it.
William Faulkner, letter to Bill Fielden

Hollywood producer Hal Wallis: What do you want to do?
William Faulkner: Go home to Mississippi.

Home… his native land; he was born of it, and his bones
will sleep in it; loving it, even while hating some of it.
William Faulkner, *Essay on Mississippi*

I discovered that my own little postage stamp of native soil was worth
writing about, and that I would never live long enough to exhaust it…
William Faulkner, *Paris Review* interview

Yes, finally somebody has done something to put
Mississippi on the map.
William Faulkner, on Mary Ann Mobley's becoming Miss America

There is one comfort; at least I can't be any sicker
tomorrow for Mississippi than I was yesterday.
William Faulkner, while living in Hollywood

We love Mississippi and its ways and customs and soil and people.
William Faulkner, letter to *Memphis Commercial Appeal*

The only way we will make progress in Mississippi
is to deal with race on a daily basis.
Andy Mullins

Mississippi has a way of trying to make
everybody look alike, think alike, act alike.
Andy Mullins

…it was the land that made you, that nourished you,
that would, eventually, claim you.
Wyatt Cooper, *Families*

We have in truth never left home, for we carry it around with us.
Wyatt Cooper, *Families*

A Mississippi of myths and legends, of fantasy about what never was
and hope for what might never be, of insufferable
baseness and incredible goodness…
Governor William Winter

In 1965, my parents broke two laws of Mississippi:
they went to Ohio to marry, returned to Mississippi.
Natasha Trethewey, *Miscegenation*

With us, when you speak of 'the river', though there be many, you
mean always the same one, the great river, the shifting, unappeasable
god of the country, feared and loved: the Mississippi.
William Alexander Percy

Why has Mississippi had such a hard time shaking its reputation?
Perhaps because Mississippi ratified the 13th Amendment
abolishing slavery 148 years late.
Jon Stewart, *The Daily Show*

Nothing in this world is a matter of black and white, not even in
Mississippi, where everything is a matter of black and white.
Richard Rubis, *Confederacy of Silence*

Spend a week or two in Tupelo, Mississippi, and you begin to wonder
if the air down here perhaps contains an element that causes dreams to
ignite and burn hotter and stranger than elsewhere in the world.
Wells Tower, *GQ* magazine

With friends around and even pals I know are true
Still I'm lonely, homesick and blue...
Longing for my Mississippi home.
Jimmie Rodgers, "Mississippi Delta Blues"

After the movie *Blood Simple*, everybody thought I was from Texas.
After *Mississippi Burning*, everybody thought I
was from Mississippi and uneducated.
Frances McDormand, actress

Alabama, also known as Liberal Mississippi.
Trevor Noah, *The Daily Show*

You can love Mississippi, but she doesn't always love you back.
David Sansing

Delmar: All my sins have been washed away, even robbing that Piggly Wiggly store.

Ulysses Everett McGill: Even if it did put you square with the Lord, the state of Mississippi is a little more hard-nosed.

O' Brother, Where Art Thou

The great state of Mississippi cannot afford four more years of Pappy O'Daniel as Governor — four more years of cronyism, nepotism, rascalism.

Homer Stokes, *O' Brother, Where Art Thou*

The two most useless things in Mississippi are Ole Miss lawyers and county agents.

Jerry Wilburn

I return to Mississippi, state that made a crime of me…

Natasha Trethewey, "Native Guard"

Roy Dale suspected that Mississippi was beautiful. He wasn't sure. He didn't have anything to compare it to. He hadn't even ever been out of the Delta.

Lewis Nordan, *Wolf Whistle*

Regardless of what happened in Medgar's life, this is and was his state. There is a degree of anger, but also a lot of love. Mississippi is home.

Myrlie Evers

We have arguably produced the best writers in the world and the worst racists.

Jim Dees, *The Statue & the Fury*

MISSISSIPPI LEGISLATURE

By a vote of one to nothing, I damn the Mississippi Legislature to Hell,
and they can stay there until I back down. They
need not plan on returning.

Hodding Carter's front page editorial following a unanimous
vote censuring Carter for his moderate stance on race

Lord help you if you are dependent on the Mississippi Legislature.

George McLean

It's boat-rocking time in Mississippi!

Governor William Winter, speech to Mississippi Legislature

The Legislature of the state of Mississippi solemnly warns Premier
Stalin of communistic Russia that its patience is exhausted.

Resolution of the Mississippi Legislature

The stars don't scrimmage.

Ellis Bodron's comment when a fellow senator criticized him for missing a meeting.

They've kept us here so long we've gone to cheating on our girlfriends.

Representative Jerry Wilburn on an extended legislative session

Well-perfumed hysteria.

Senator Ellis Bodron's comment about the women advocating kindergartens in 1982

These lobbyists are trying to create a monotony.

Mississippi legislator's malaprop

On the ominous pay bill before us, let me note that this pay raise is so
important, we need to make it radioactive.

Mississippi legislator's malaprops during discussion of a pay raise for state workers.

That's a good bill, but it's no pancreas.

Mississippi legislator's malaprop

If it's one thing we need *clearification* on, it is how to
clearify that section of the code.

Mississippi legislator's malaprop

I'm a walking encyclopedia on these matters.
State Senator Steve Holland

Let me just make one comment — and then I'm
going to make another comment.
Representative Manly Barton

The chairman has informed me I don't have enough hair to talk about
the cosmetologists, but I believe this is the sorriest agency in state
government. This board's a rotten mess, a tee-total rotten mess.
Representative Steve Holland, on the State Board of Cosmetology

I've never seen anything like it. I'm inclined to offer a constitutional
amendment to prohibit the Legislature from
convening during election years.
Senator Hob Bryan, on election-year pandering

Son, I just need to know one thing. Did anybody take
what wasn't his and run off with it?
Senator Bill Harpole to investigator after a complex
and lengthy briefing on a criminal matter

As a freshman legislator, Steve Holland was young, brash, and cocky.
The only difference today is that he's no longer young..
Danny Miller

Thirty hissing possums in a barn.
Saturday Night Live's description of the Mississippi legislature

If this bill passes, everyone will want to vote.
Legislator to John Grisham, who was advocating for a mail-in voter
registration bill before the Mississippi House of Representatives

Are you kidding me? Why are we even considering a bill to
spend $1.2 million on Dick Molpus' image?
Senator Brad Lott, misunderstanding the bill under consideration, which was to
computerize all documents in the secretary of state's office through imaging

Steve Holland is a gloriously profane and paradoxically genteel man.
Wells Tower, *GQ* Magazine

I can absolutely make love to a bull moose on the steps of the Lee
County courthouse and garner more than five percent of the vote.
Steve Holland

You've got to get your ass up early and go to bed late to beat my ass.
Steve Holland

After losing that third time, Governor Winter had to feel like,
my gosh, this is the worst job in the world.
Ed Perry, on the multiple defeats of Governor William Winter's education reforms

If knowledge were a prerequisite for speech, there would be a lot of
silence in the Mississippi State Senate.
Senator Ellis Bodron

State Senator: The gentleman has cast aspirations on me.
State Senator Theodore Smith: I can assure my colleague
that I would never cast aspirations on him, for I'm sure
he has none.

Voting on this bill has got me caught
between raising hell and amazing grace.
Representative Lynn Havens

If you have a deep need for love, don't run
for the Mississippi Legislature.
Walter "Squirrel" Phillips

It looks to me like the winds of change have turned into a tornado.
Speaker Buddie Newman

Mr. Speaker, this is the last time I'm going to
speak against something I'm for.
Representative Butch Lambert

That's the last time I'm voting for a bill I'm against.
Representative Bruce Hansen, on the 1982 Education Reform Act

MONEY

If you got money, that place will fix any man's blues.
Paul "Wine" Jones, on a Memphis whorehouse

If you're so smart, why ain't you rich?
Eudora Welty

While I have to write trash, I don't care who buys it, as
long as they pay the best price I can get.
William Faulkner

If I ever need the money badly enough, I'll do some more movie work.
William Faulkner

Let's take the money and haul ass.
John Grisham, *The Firm*

They pay me real good money to stay worried.
John Grisham, *The Firm*

I worship money.
John Grisham, *The Summons*

Anyone could be bought.
John Grisham, *The Summons*

I ain't broke, but I'm badly bent. Everybody
wants them dead presidents.
Willie Dixon, *Dead Presidents*

Times are hard; money is scarce, prices low, and business dull.
Congressman "Private" John Allen

Blanche: I took the trip as an investment, thinking I'd meet
someone with a million dollars.
Tennessee Williams, *A Streetcar Named Desire*

It certainly has come a long way in a year.
Billy Mounger, II, on a merger of his company that created
$5 billion in equity on a $180 million investment.

It cost eleven dollars. It must be good.
Kathryn Stockett, *The Help*

If you have an extra dollar, give fifty cents to someone who needs it
more than you — with the remainder, buy a book.
Neil White, *In the Sanctuary of Outcasts*, quoting his great-grandmother Floy

How the devil did Grand scrape together $250 in these times of
famine? For ways that are dark and tricks that are vain…
I almost suspect her of embezzling church funds.
Tennessee Williams, letter to his mother

Capital has no conscience. I don't believe
a man ever made a million honestly.
James K. Vardaman

I have no use for bodyguards, but I have very specific use for
two highly-trained certified public accountants.
Elvis Presley

I had no idea that being your authentic self could make me as
rich as I've become. If I had, I'd have done it a lot earlier.
Oprah Winfrey

…in Natchez, people will forgive you for
everything except going bankrupt.
Greg Iles, *Natchez Burning*

In America, the rich man tries to pretend that the poor man is
his equal in every respect but money, which is simply not true.
Donna Tartt, *The Secret History*

In studying your case, I came across a passage by Scottish theologian
William Barclay. The Romans had a proverb which said that
money was like seawater. The more you drink, the thirstier you
become. In looking back at your situation, I think that's
certainly applicable, and it's sad.
Judge Glen Davidson

When we die, if there's a dollar left, it's because I've miscalculated.
Jim Barksdale

I'm not going to deceive myself for one minute that this (dropping the Rebel flag) is about making black students happy. It's about dollars.
Monique Brown, Ole Miss Black Student Union President

The theory was simple: If a man had enough sense to accumulate a bunch of cash, then he would certainly make a worthy U.S. Senator.
John Grisham, *The Client*

MULES

Some Homer of the cotton fields should sing the saga of the mule and of his place in the South. [The mule] …taught [the South] pride again through humility and courage through adversity overcome; who accomplished the well-nigh impossible despite hopeless odds, by sheer and vindictive patience.

William Faulkner, *Sartoris*

Abbeville is now so poor that few of its inhabitants can afford to buy a mule with which to till the depleted soil.

Mississippi WPA Guide

A mule is an animal that will work for you for twenty years just for the chance to kick you once.

William Faulkner, *The Reivers*

I think Faulkner loved mules almost as much as people, maybe more.

Shelby Foote

MUSIC

Rock and roll music, if you like it, if you feel it, you can't help
but move to it. That's what happens to me. I can't help it.
Elvis Presley

I sing what I have to say.
Leontyne Price

I spent fifteen minutes writing 'Stand by Your Man'
and a lifetime defending it.
Tammy Wynette

I don't know anything about music. In my line, you don't have to.
Elvis Presley

Rhythm is something you either have or don't have, but
when you have it, you have it all over.
Elvis Presley

People ask me where I got my singing style.
I didn't copy my style from anybody.
Elvis Presley

A live concert to me is exciting because of all the electricity
that is generated in the crowd and on stage. It's my
favorite part of the business, live concerts.
Elvis Presley

I learned how important it is to entertain people and give
them a reason to come and watch you play.
Elvis Presley

I've never written a song in my life. It's all a big hoax.
Elvis Presley

What are you doin'?
Record Producer Sam Philips to an unknown Elvis Presley when
Phillips overheard Elvis singing "That's Alright, Mama" to himself

The colored folks been singing it and playing it just like I'm doin' now, man, for more years than I know. I got it from them.

Elvis Presley

I happened to come along in the music
business when there was no trend.

Elvis Presley

I like entertaining people. I really miss it.

Elvis Presley

I like to sing ballads… but the way I'm singing
now is what makes the money.

Elvis Presley

I sure lost my musical direction in Hollywood. My songs were the same conveyer belt mass production, just like most of my movies were.

Elvis Presley

I miss my singing career very much.

Elvis Presley

I'm no hillbilly singer.

Elvis Presley

Man, that record came out and was real big. Don't
know why — the lyrics had no meaning.

Elvis Presley

I hate to get started in these jam sessions. I'm
always the last one to leave.

Elvis Presley

In memory, everything seems to happen to music.

Tennessee Williams

Some writers are curiously unmusical. I don't get it.
I don't get them. For me, music is essential.

Barry Hannah

Man, you don't know how I felt that afternoon when I
heard that voice and it was my own voice.
Muddy Waters

You get a heck of a sound from the church.
Can't you hear it in my voice?
Muddy Waters

I rambled all the time. I was just like that, like a rollin' stone.
Muddy Waters

My grandmother, she says I shouldn't be playing. I should go to church.
Muddy Waters

I wanted definitely to be a musician or a good preacher or a heck of a
baseball player. I couldn't play ball too good. I couldn't preach,
and, well, all I had left was getting into the music thing.
Muddy Waters

I was always singing the way I felt.
Muddy Waters

It seems like I always had to work harder than other people.
Those nights when everybody else is asleep, and you
sit in your room trying to play scales.
B.B. King

There are so many sounds I still want to make,
so many things I haven't yet done.
B.B. King

If you can't get your songs to people one way, you have to find another.
B.B. King

The ghosts from the old house — Caruso, Flagstad — were
saying to me, 'Lee, you mess up and we'll take care of you.'
Leontyne Price, on her first performance at the new Metropolitan Opera House

It was the first operatic mountain I climbed, and the
view from it was astounding, exhilarating, stupefying.
Leontyne Price, on her 1961 Metropolitan Opera debut

No one comes to this end of Elvis Presley
Boulevard anymore. Only the devout.
Ace Atkins, *Crossroad Blues*

NATURE

The fish aren't biting, but the mosquitos are.
Rick Bass, *Wild to the Heart.*

Nature does not like to be anticipated... but loves to surprise.
Walter Anderson

...art and nature are literally one thing.
Walter Anderson

Sometimes... a vacuum is a hell of a lot better than
some of the stuff that nature replaces it with.
Tennessee Williams, *Cat on a Hot Tin Roof*

The night screamed with its birds and frogs and bugs.
Tom Franklin, *Crooked Letter, Crooked Letter*

A mockingbird can imitate anything, even a truck grinding gears.
William Faulkner

...the lush green of summer and the regal blaze of fall and the
rain and ruin of winter before spring would bloom again.
William Faulkner, *Sepulture South*

The fireflies — lightning bugs of the Mississippi child's vernacular —
myriad and frenetic, random and frantic, pulsing; not
questing, but quiring, but choiring as if they were tiny
incessant appeaseless voices, cries, words.
William Faulkner, *The Town*

And the nights, bigger than imagining; black and gusty
and enormous, disordered and wild with stars.
Donna Tartt, *The Secret History*

Just take off your glasses, the plants will look great.
Felder Rushing, *The Gestalt Gardner*, when a lady asked
what to do about brown spots on her plants

Fire ants in your garden make you garden faster.
Felder Rushing

If the old black ladies down by the river are still sitting on their bait buckets, it's still too cold to plant your tomatoes.
Felder Rushing

Summer tomatoes are one of the few joys of August; a succulent air pocket in the ring of fire.
Jim Dees, *Lies and Other Truths*

Camille came, and the wind sounded like trains.
Jesmyn Ward, *Salvage the Bones*

NEWS MEDIA

Whatever endangers freedom of speech and of the press
directly endangers every other advantage of a free society.
Hodding Carter, *Where Main Street Meets the River*

A true newspaper man spends his life wanting to see and to tell.
Turner Catledge, *My Life at the Times*

There is a key measurement of how far we have come. In the 1960s,
the phone lines between the governor's mansion and the *Clarion Ledger*
newspaper were used to promote segregation. In 1982, those same
phone lines were used to promote education and bring people together.
Charles Overby

Today, everybody can be a journalist, but not everybody is credible.
Ed Meek

A while back, I spent three years in prison. I just got out of a six-hour
board of education meeting. Three years in prison was
easy by comparison.
Slim Smith, *Columbus Dispatch* columnist

Reporters are an agile lot.
Governor Ray Mabus, when his public safety commissioner
inadvertently bumped a gaggle of reporters crowded around her car

I bought a bankrupt newspaper from a bankrupt bank in Tupelo,
Mississippi, in the most bankrupt time in American history.
George McLean

Bert, I'm going to whip your ass.
Governor Kirk Fordice to WLBT newsman Bert Case

As to the reports in newspapers, we must scorn them, else they will ruin
us and our country. They are as much enemies to good government
as the secessionists, and between the two I like the secessionists best,
because they are a brave, open enemy and not a set of
sneaking, croaking scoundrels.
General William Tecumpseh Sherman's comment on the news media at Vicksburg

The 'Yank' correspondents, as gifted and individualistic and
undisciplined and courageously enterprising a group of
American newspapermen as ever lived.
Hodding Carter, *Where Main Street Meets the River*

Among my odder keepsakes is a letter from
Boss Crump. It is not a love letter.
Hodding Carter, *Where Main Street Meets the River*

The only way you can get along with newspapermen is to be like Dizzy
Dean. Say something one minute and something different the next.
Hank Greenberg, on Dizzy Dean

Hell, that's what the news is — an emergency.
Turner Catledge, *My Life at the Times*

This meeting is adjourned.
Turner Catledge, four-word speech delivered after a series
of lengthy orations. Catledge received a standing ovation.

The University of Texas Regents are as much concerned with free
intellectual enterprise as a razorback sow would be with
Keat's 'Ode on a Grecian Urn.'
Historian J. Frank Dobie defending Willie Morris, who was attacked by the
UT Regents for his outspoken advocacy as editor of *The Daily Texan*

Hodding Carter is unfit to live in decent white society.
Speaker Walter Sillers

You have some good qualities, but you
will never make a newspaper man.
***Associated Press* supervisor** firing Hodding Carter

Television news is like a lightning flash. It makes a loud noise,
lights up everything around it, leaves everthing else in
darkness, and then is suddenly gone.
Hodding Carter

Muckraker, ball-buster, force of nature, cat lover, red-wine-please, bitch.
Description of Lucy Morgan, by Lucy Morgan

I've been getting some bad publicity — but you got to expect that.
Elvis Presley

Trenchant editorials, plus the keen rivalry natural to extremely
partisan papers, made it necessary for the editors to be
expert pugilists and duelists, as well as journalists.
Mississippi WPA Guide

For newspapers, free is not a business model.
Charles Overby

Good intentions often go astray. There is a fine line between doing
something for somebody and doing something to somebody.
Charles Overby

Southern journalists and politicians have shaped our country's destiny
from its beginning, for better and for worse. Their passions and
principles, their vigor and style have made our region
formidable, tragic, mythic and historic.
Charles Overby.

Trash cans are very useful things.
Bill Beckwith, on newspaper stories

I had seen enough press events to know that when the
TV camera light goes on, reality flies out the window.
Jim Dees, *The Statue & the Fury*

...if that pissed off the mayor, well, that was a good day at the office.
Jim Dees, *The Statue & the Fury*

Objective journalism is tooth fairy stuff. Journalism is as
objective as the human beings who write it.
Jim Dees, *The Statue & the Fury*

OLE MISS & OXFORD

I got hypnotized one day by this girl who
was going to school over at Ole Miss.
Larry Brown, *Dirty Work*

Isn't that what you women from Ole Miss major in?
Professional husband hunting?
Kathryn Stockett, *The Help*

'Going from Hilly to Celia must've been quite the change, Johnny.'
Johnny shakes his head… 'Like going to bed in a
seminary and waking up at Ole Miss.'
Kathryn Stockett, *The Help*

Hound Dog Hurley's main claim to fame was having to
take twelve years to graduate from Ole Miss.
Gayden Metcalfe, *Being Dead is No Excuse*

Oh, you go to Ole Miss.
Response of Ole Miss alumnus when told his friend
attended The University of the South

Question: What is the biggest difference at Ole Miss from the
1950s when you were a student and Ole Miss today?
Answer: The legs on the women.
Chancellor Robert Khayat

Sheriff Dennis lifts an Ole Miss coffee mug off the desk and spits
tobacco juice into it. 'I like spitting on the Rebels,' he says distractedly.
Greg Iles, *Natchez Burning*

…the actual boys I knew at Ole Miss, passionless frat boys whose
hearts had already narrowed and tightened into the hearts of the
burghers and businessmen they would someday become.
Donna Tartt

I felt sorry for all these millions of people here
(New York City) because they don't live in Oxford.
William Faulkner

…My whole town [Oxford] spent much of its time trying to decide just what living man I was writing about, the one literary criticism of the town being, 'How in hell did he remember all that, and when did that happen anyway?'
William Faulkner

No writer had a greater sense of place than William Faulkner. But I don't know what Faulkner was writing about. I was in Oxford, Mississippi, recently, and Oxford is one of the nicest places I've ever visited. It is nothing like the backwater town Faulkner described in his novels.
Englishman's remarks following a visit to Oxford

Oxford Town in the afternoon
Ev'rybody singin a sorrowful tune
Two men died 'neath the Mississippi Moon
Somebody better investigate soon.
Bob Dylan, "Oxford Town"

Oxford is the literary capital of Mississippi. It may well be the literary capital of America.
David Crews

I don't live in Mississippi. I live in Oxford.
Unknown

Not many towns of 10,000 can claim a Nobel Prize winner in Literature.
Jim Dees, *The Statue & the Fury*

…we kick off the Faulkner Centennial with a fussy small-town controversy featuring an enormously heavy statue of the great little man, a magnolia removed by midnight execution, and a tyrannical mayor.
Jim Dees, *The Statue & the Fury*

PARCHMAN

It's Parchman… destination doom.
William Faulkner, *The Mansion*

Judge gave me life this morning, down on Parchman Farm.
Bluesman Bukka White

Well I'm putting that cotton in an eleven-foot sack,
with a twelve-gauge shotgun at my back.
Mose Allison

Parchman was so big, isolated, and remote — 18,000 flat and virtually
treeless acres in the middle of Delta nowhere — that it had never
needed fences. Where could a prisoner run to? Where could he hide
where the bloodhounds wouldn't find him? He was
imprisoned by space, emptiness, and distance.
Richard Grant, *Dispatches from Pluto*

Parchman… the days were long down there
when you had a hoe in your hands.
Larry Brown, *Father and Son*

He's in the jail house now. He's in the jailhouse now.
Jimmie Rodgers, "In the Jailhouse Now"

POKER

Deaf or no deaf, he can hear a fifty-dollar
raise if you don't even move your lips.
William Faulkner, *Race At Morning*

Army life is pretty dull in peacetime: nothing to do but lay around
and lie your head off all day and play poker all night.
William Faulkner, *Honor*

What little of psychology I know, the characters I have invented and
playing poker have taught me. Freud, I'm not familiar with.
William Faulkner, to UVA medical class

Poker shouldn't be played in a house with women.
Tennessee Williams, *A Streetcar Named Desire*

POLITICS

I never made popularity the standard of my action.
L.Q.C. Lamar

I'm not ashamed of having gone to jail, for I remember that St. Paul,
that great soldier of the Cross, went to jail. It was also while serving
a prison sentence that John Bunyan wrote *Pilgrim's Progress*... Yes, my
friends, Bilbo went to jail and Bilbo is proud of his company.
Theodore G. Bilbo

Senator John Stennis, a decent small-town judge, who had,
amid general rejoicing, succeeded Bilbo in the senate.
Hodding Carter, *Where Main Street Meets the River*

The camera is a natural attraction for a politician. And if a camera is
here, we're going to be here. And we're going to say
something, even if we have nothing to say.
Thad Cochran, on permitting TV coverage of senate debates, *New York Times*

My aunt... like many well-born Southern ladies,
embraced advanced political ideas.
Walker Percy, *The Moviegoer*

Between Barbarism and Wall Street, I think he
rather leans toward Barbarism.
LeRoy Percy, on Vardaman

We assumed that, being a Republican, he
was bound to be an atheist too.
Turner Catledge, *My Life at the Times*

The only thing that protected Republicans
in the South was the game laws.
Turner Catledge, *My Life at the Times*

There often comes a time in a statesman's life when he must
rise above principle and take a stand for his people.
Congressman Percy Quin

All of you who were generals, vote for General Tucker ...and all of you who were privates, vote for me, "Private" John Allen.

Congressman "Private" John Allen

We are not contemplating any effort to move the capitol in Washington to Tupelo, however advantageous it might be to the capitol.

Congressman "Private" John Allen

Exchange in congressional campaign:

W.B. Walker: Gentlemen, I want you to notice my opponent, Mr. Allen. Just look at him sitting over there, big and fat. Why, he's literally pregnant on the people's money, he has been in Congress so long.

Congressman "Private" John Allen, while patting his stomach: When I am in labor and delivered of this child, if it's a girl I will name it Martha Washington. If it's a boy, I will name it George Washington. And if it's a jackass, I will name it W.B. Walker.

He has ricommended hisself so much higher than any of the rest of us kin ricommend him.

Congressman "Private" John Allen, referring to a political opponent

Some senators grow, and others simply swell. Make sure you grow.

Senator John Stennis to new U.S. Senators

I will plow a straight furrow to the end of my row.

Senator John Stennis

I walked down enough furrows and turn rows to chop forty acres of cotton.

Congressman Frank Smith, on how far he walked campaigning door to door

All members of Congress have a primary interest in being re-elected. Some members have no other interest.

Congressman Frank Smith

There are almost as many definitions of integrity as there are members of Congress.

Congressman Frank Smith

The Jew-nited Nations.

Congressman John Rankin's description of the United Nations

The DAR leaders were rabid activists who responded
with alarm to every breeze that shook a branch.

Congressman Frank Smith

I didn't know my family was that big.

Governor Haley Barbour, on his 3% national poll
ranking for President, *Meet the Press*

Ross Barnett's smile is as astonishing and repelling
as a grin on the face of a vulture.

Ira B. Harkey, Jr., *Pascagoula Chronicle*

Ross Barnett is an inflexible racist with a mind relatively innocent of
history, constitutional law, and the processes of government.

James Silver

The fire of his Robesperian oratory was heard by one of
the largest gatherings since the last hanging.

Newspaper comment on James K. Vardaman

The main thing is to keep the main thing the main thing.

Governor Haley Barbour

If you don't like Haley Barbour, you've got something wrong with you.

Ed Gillespie, Republican strategist

Haley Barbour is the Midas of political fundraisers.

Andrew Ferguson, *The Weekly Standard*

The Barbour style of pronunciation involves a fatal collision of sibilants,
as if he'd left the dentist's office before the Novocain could wear off.

Andrew Ferguson, *The Weekly Standard*

You don't have to be a Midwestern weenie to imagine Haley Barbour as
the Southern sheriff in *Deliverance*, squinting at Jon Voight
through aviator sunglasses and suggesting he might
want to get his pale Yankee ass out of town.

Andrew Ferguson, *The Weekly Standard*

I want to be majority leader of the Senate mighty bad,
but not bad enough to ask Bilbo for his vote.

Senator Pat Harrison; Harrison lost the powerful post
by one vote, with Bilbo voting against him.

I had a few lumps, bruises, and heartaches in my political career.

J.P. Coleman

I don't think you can tell anything about anybody running for political
office by looking at him on TV. I want to look him in the eye and feel
his right hand and see if he impresses me up close and not
just under the glitter of television and makeup.

J.P. Coleman

Mississippi has had its fair share of buffoons and demagogues.

J.P. Coleman

**Young lawyer from New Hampshire, in letter to his
uncle in Mississippi**: I would like to come down to
Mississippi to practice law. In politics I am a Republican
and personally I am an honest man. What chance will I
have in Mississippi?

The uncle: By all means come. As a Republican the game laws
will protect you. And if you are an honest man, you
won't have any competition among the Republicans.

Despite all my success, I feel confident to administer a word of caution.
Do not be deceived by the glitter of public office. My greatest regret is
that I ever made a political speech or held a political office.

Albert Gallatin Brown, who served as governor, senator,
and congressman from Mississippi

There are those who think that by loud noises, waving of arms, and
stomping of feet, our public officials and leaders can drive the evil spirit
of integration away. Political quackery is just as imbecilic as medicinal
quackery… Only intelligence and straight thinking can save us.

Armis Hawkins, in speech during unsuccessful campaign for lieutenant governor

Richard Nixon cares no more about Mississippi
than he does for a swamp rat.

Armis Hawkins

Children attending Head Start live (in an environment) so bad they
would be better off sitting up on a piano bench in a whorehouse.
Governor Haley Barbour, during 2003 gubernatorial campaign.

Perhaps Mr. Barbour will enlighten us on his first-hand knowledge of
what goes on inside a whorehouse, especially one with a piano.
Armis Hawkins, in response to Governor Barbour's
comments about Head Start and whorehouses

We shall not rest until demagogues like you are
driven from the political arena of Mississippi.
Medgar Evers to gubernatorial candidate Paul Johnson, Jr.

There is little point in the people electing public officials
if the officials cease to be public once they are elected.
Hodding Carter editorial in the *Delta Democrat Times*, regarding secret
proceedings of the IHL Board on Medgar Evers' application to Ole Miss

I'm running for first lady, and I'm unopposed.
Republican gubernatorial candidate, Leon Bramlett's, wife, highlighting the
fact that Democratic candidate, Bill Allain, was divorced

When Strom Thurmond ran for President, Mississippians voted for
him. And if the rest of the country had followed our lead, we wouldn't
have had all these problems over the years either.
Senator Trent Lott

We will have on our program the person who is going
to stick the knife in Senator Trent Lott's back.
George Stephanopoulos on ABC's *This Week* news program, in reference to
Senator Don Nickles and efforts to remove Lott as senate majority leader

Throw the bums in.
Ron Shapiro, candidate for mayor of Oxford, MS

Elect me, and I'll spend less time with my family.
Ron Shapiro's slogan for Oxford alderman campaign

How's the campaign going, and don't tell me anything good.
Rogers Varner, who had already suffered through two previous
defeats supporting his brother-in-law, William Winter

I'm a lobbyist, and had a career lobbying. The guy or lady who gets elected President of the U.S. will immediately be lobbying: advocating to Congress, lobbying our allies and adversaries overseas.
Governor Haley Barbour

The Obama administration and the Democratic Congress have taken the biggest lurch to the left in American history.
Governor Haley Barbour

Finch Rhymes with Wrench
Governor Cliff Finch's campaign slogan

Stand Tall for Paul
Governor Paul Johnson's campaign slogan

Roll with Ross
Governor Ross Barnett's campaign slogan

Fight to Win for Mississippi: Win with Winter
Governor William Winter's 1967 campaign slogan

Winter for Governor: The Toughest Job in Mississippi
Governor William Winter's 1979 campaign slogan

Make a Cross for Jim Buck Ross
Agricultural Commissioner Jim Buck Ross' campaign slogan

A Straight Shooter
Convicted murderer Byron de la Beckwith's campaign slogan

Me & My Truck Are for Amy Tuck
Lieutenant Governor Amy Tuck's bumper sticker slogan

Compromise is the key to survival.
Senator Trent Lott

Southerners who broke from the Democratic Party like some renegade strain of amoeba and took over the body politic of the GOP.
Curtis Wilkie, *George Magazine*

The spirit of Jefferson Davis lives in the 1984 Republican platform.
Curtis Wilkie

I'd rather be a hound dog in Mississippi than spend
another term in the U.S. Senate.
Senator John Sharp Williams

There's only two ways to run for office: unopposed or worried.
Mayor Bill Luckett

He reminded us of our duties and responsibilities if
we wished to continue as a nation.
William Faulkner, on Abraham Lincoln

A Republican is a man who made his money; a liberal is a man who
inherited his; a Democrat is a barefooted liberal in a cross-country race;
a conservative is a Republican who has learned to read and write.
William Faulkner, *The Reivers*

Huey Long in Louisiana had made himself founder, owner, and
supporter of one of the best literary magazines anywhere,
without ever once looking inside it.
William Faulkner, *Knight's Gambit*

Adlai Stevenson had three strikes against
him: wit, urbanity, and erudition.
William Faulkner

I'm strictly for Adlai Stevenson. I don't dig the intellectual
bit, but I'm telling you, man, he knows the most.
Elvis Presley

I'm a William Winter Democrat and a Jack Reed Republican.
Billy Crews

The secret of success as a political consultant is to work for candidates
who were going to win anyway and not screw it up.
Stuart Stevens, *The Last Season*

…Our big candied yam of a governor.
Richard Ford, *Let Me Be Frank with You*

Any person who wants to govern the world is, by
definition, the wrong person to do it.
Greg Iles

1st voter: What do you think about that young fellow, William
Winter?
2nd voter: Don't vote for him; he's a liberal.
1st voter: What's a liberal?
2nd voter: Well, he's a N-lover.
I overheard these two gentlemen, and I thought
to myself, 'William Winter's my man.'
Rueben Anderson, commenting on conversation he
overheard in the 1967 gubernatorial election

Politics has its place, but politics should
never get in the way of good policy.
Governor Haley Barbour

I've determined that three things are going to happen in this business
climate. You will innovate; you will immigrate, or you will evaporate.
Governor Haley Barbour

After I got that DUI, I found out there were twenty-two Baptist
churches in my district. So I ended up rededicating
my life seventeen times during June and July.
Representative Lynn Havens

The Yellow Dog Democrats were strangled by both Republicans
and Democrats, and became Blue Dog Democrats.
Representative Sonny Montgomery

I have nothing against Senator Cochran. I just want his job.
James "Booty" Hunt, perennial candidate for the U.S. Senate

Watching the Democratic and Republican presidential primaries, and the absolute orgy of anger and irrational behavior conducted in the name of "liberty" and "freedom," it has become obvious to me that the days of disagreeing agreeably over politics in America are approaching what is perhaps a permanent sunset.

Sid Salter, on 2016 Presidential campaign

There is an intrinsic value in the governor of a small, poor state knowing exactly what relief to request and to whom to make that request…. That was Haley Barbour's great gift as Mississippi governor in times of crisis. Barbour was a force of nature in Jackson, more often than not winning political battles that he didn't have the constitutional power as governor to win.

Sid Salter

He's a two-faced, cutthroat, dirt-dumb, chicken shit, slimy, little bastard with a bright future in politics.

John Grisham, *The Testament*

The Mississippi Legislature went to great lengths to do nothing.

Senator Hob Bryan

We need to pass this bill, so we can tell what's in it.

Rep. Gary Chism

I gladly charge Republicans double so I can bury Democrats for free.

Steve Holland, Undertaker and State Representative

PRIVACY

I am working tooth and nail at my lifetime ambition to be the last private individual on Earth, and expect every success, since, apparently, there is no competition for the place.
William Faulkner, letter to Hamilton Basso

…one of the most fearful things in modern American life: the Freedom of the Press.
William Faulkner, on the news media's intrusion on his privacy

…please warn him (*Time* magazine journalist) that I will be dug in to defend what remains of my privacy to the last bullet.
William Faulkner, letter to Don Klopfer

Let me write the books. Let someone who wants it have the publicity. I protest the whole idea, but will never consent to my picture on cover. Estimate what refusal will cost Random House, and I will pay it.
William Faulkner, telegram to Bennett Cerf expressing opposition to a *Time* magazine cover story

I like Virginia and I like Virginians. Virginians are all snobs, and I like snobs. A snob has to spend so much time being a snob that he has little time left to meddle with you.
William Faulkner, press conference at UVA

You should put a blank record in the juke box so I can buy three minutes of silence.
William Faulkner to owner of Mistilis Cafe

I'm too old at my age to travel that far to eat with strangers.
William Faulkner, on declining an invitation to dine with President Kennedy

What a commentary; Sweden gave me the Nobel Prize. France gave me the Legion d'Honneur. All my native land did for me was to invade my privacy over my protest and my plea.
William Faulkner, letter to Phil Mullen

Donna Tartt is that rare thing, the last private
woman in the world of the selfie.
Unknown

To really be centered, and to really work well, and to think
about the kinds of things that I need to think about, I
need to spend large amounts of time alone.
Donna Tartt

Writing is a lonely business.
Donna Tartt

My age and my face are mine, and I refuse,
emphatically, to have them published in *Life*.
Maude Falkner, on her privacy

He detested more than anything the invasion of his privacy.
William Styron, on William Faulkner, *Life* Magazine, July 1962

My private life is my private life — my books are in the
public domain — and there's no connection.
William Faulkner to columnist Earl Wilson

If you got something you don't want other people
to know, keep it in your pocket.
Muddy Waters

My relatives were private people, building walls not only to
shield themselves from outsiders but from one another.
Dean Faulkner Wells, *Every Day by the Sun*

PROGRESS

Clever willful machines… moving without comprehensible
purpose toward no discernible destination.
William Faulkner, from review of Jimmy Collins' book *Test Pilot*

…our whole modern economy of waste.
William Faulkner, letter to *New York Times* (never sent)

RELIGION

There were men in Neshoba County so religious they would
ask the blessing before they took a chew of tobacco.
Clayton Rand

I'm giving up Mississippi for Lent.
Anonymous, quoted in *The Courting of Marcus Dupree*

It was impossible to be from Mississippi
and not be familiar with churches.
Jack Butler, *Jujitsu for Christ*

He wasn't a Christian, or maybe he was, but if he was, he
wasn't the kind of Christian that people who call
themselves Christians would call a Christian.
Jack Butler, *Jujitsu for Christ*

God don't cause no shit like that to happen.
Larry Brown, *Dirty Work*

He (God) ain't responsible for all that…
Man does all this stuff to himself.
Larry Brown, *Dirty Work*, on killing in war

I knew that somewhere, Jesus wept.
Larry Brown, *Dirty Work*

I'm praying to the Lord and the devil on the side.
Kathryn Stockett, *The Help*

Colored people attend too much church.
Kathryn Stockett, *The Help*

There is nothing finer than a group of people
meeting in true Christian fellowship.
Ross Barnett speaking to Jewish congregation

Historically, Methodists are better behaved than Episcopalians.
Gayden Metcalfe, *Being Dead Is No Excuse*

Methodists are frustrated Baptists who'd like to be Episcopalians.
Lucy Mattie Trigg

If God wasn't mightily amused by our humanness, I
figure he'd have wiped us out a long time ago.
Jill Connor Browne

How many folks you think'd be in churches on
Sundays ef the hippie-crits stayed home?
Armis Hawkins, *The Grand Leader*

Bein' a Christian don't mean you got to chunk
all the sense you got out the winder.
Armis Hawkins, *The Grand Leader*

Uncle May… was a one-man longitude on religious stuff.
Armis Hawkins, *The Grand Leader*

Since I was raised a Presbyterian, pretty much all pleasures are guilty.
Richard Ford

Until we meet again, may God bless you as He has blessed me.
Elvis Presley

You ain't got to. You can't help it. And He knows that. But
you can suffer. And He knows that too. He don't tell
you not to sin, He just asks you not to.
William Faulkner, on sin

God… is the most complete expression of mankind.
William Faulkner to Loic Bouvard

Well, whatever one thinks of the Roman Church, it is a worthy and
powerful foe. I could accept that sort of conversion with grace. But I
shall be very disappointed indeed if we lose him to the Presbyterians.
Donna Tartt, *The Secret History*

We're talking about God here. God is serious business.
Donna Tartt, *The Secret History*

I am deeply skeptical of those in politics who flaunt their religion in their political pursuits. I have seen my share of charlatans who brazenly trafficked in religious rhetoric to further their own interests.
Governor William Winter

...the polls report that 98% of Americans believe in God and the remaining 2% are atheists and agnostics — which leaves not a single percentage point for a seeker.
Walker Percy, *The Moviegoer*

To the mind that could dream and shape our beaconed universe, what is injustice to us may be unfathomable tenderness, and our horror only loveliness misunderstood.
William Alexander Percy

Maybe God changed as the individual changed, or perhaps grew as one grew.
Anne Moody, *Coming of Age in Mississippi*

Jesus preached more and taught more about helping the poor and the sick and the hungry than he did about heaven and hell. Shouldn't that tell us something?
John Grisham

I think it's time to throw the snake out into the congregation!
Steve Holland

What we Baptists call sin, you Methodists call fellowship.
Steve Holland

SACRIFICE

…liberty gained without honor and sacrifice and held without constant vigilance and undiminished honor and complete willingness to sacrifice again at need, was not worth having to begin with.
William Faulkner, *An Innocent at Rinkside*

Liberty and freedom not given man as a free gift, but as a right and responsibility to be earned if he deserves it, is worthy of it, is willing to work for it by means of courage and sacrifice, and then to defend it always.
William Faulkner, *To the Youth of Japan*

…the old verities and truths of the heart… love and honor and pity and pride and compassion and sacrifice.
William Faulkner, Nobel Prize address

SEX

Have you thought about children? It requires sex, remember?
John Grisham, *The Firm*

John doesn't write much about sex, perhaps because
John doesn't know that much about sex.
Renee Grisham, humorous response to question about
why there is very little sex in her husband's novels

Were you intimate with her? I suppose so.
Though intimate is not quite the word.
Walker Percy, *The Moviegoer*

Not a bad life! Drink well, eat well, and make love to Margot.
Walker Percy, *Lancelot*

I had the dimmest notion of how children were born, though
I knew it required a little cooperation.
William Alexander Percy, *Lanterns on the Levee*

We gonna pitch a wang dang doodle, all night long.
Willie Dixon, "Wang Dang Doodle"

All of 'em ain't my wife's. She had two, and the
balance I got jest frolickin' around.
Holt Collier, on his 14 children

Always wear pretty underwear, on account of you just never know.
Jill Conor Browne, *The Sweet Potato Queens Book of Love*

I'm not trying to be sexy. It's just my way of
expressing myself when I move around.
Elvis Presley

Just be nice to the gentlemen, Fancy. They'll be nice to you.
Bobbie Gentry, "Fancy"

…they made their slow, sweet love. The iron bed sounded like a pine forest in an ice storm, like a switch track in a Memphis trainyard…
Lewis Nordan, *Wolf Whistle*

Strippers…. They were an expensive habit, but one he could not break.
John Grisham, *The Client*

SUCCESS

…our success depended on every person on the
team being invested in our mission.
Robert Khayat, *The Education of a Lifetime*

…perhaps one of the things wrong with our country is success.
That there is too much success in it. Success is too easy.
William Faulkner, National Book Award address

Lots of people want to ride with you in the limo, but what you want is
someone who will take the bus with you when the limo breaks down.
Oprah Winfrey

The Lord can give, and the Lord can take away.
I might be herding sheep next year.
Elvis Presley

From the time I was a kid, I always knew something was
going to happen to me. Didn't know exactly what.
Elvis Presley

I never expected to be anybody important.
Elvis Presley

There are too many people that depend on me.
I'm too obligated. I'm in too far to get out.
Elvis Presley

They put me on television. And the whole thing
broke loose. It was wild, I tell ya for sure.
Elvis Presley

Since the beginning, it was just the same. The only
difference, the crowds are bigger now.
Elvis Presley

Those people in New York are not gonna change me none.
Elvis Presley

I was an overnight sensation.
Elvis Presley

I was training to be an electrician. I suppose I got wired the
wrong way 'round somewhere along the line.
Elvis Presley

Man, I really like Las Vegas.
Elvis Presley

I'll never make it, it will never happen, because they're never
going to hear me 'cause they're screaming all the time.
Elvis Presley

I still have my feet on the ground; I just wear better shoes.
Oprah Winfrey

Success is shy — it won't come out while you're watching.
Tennessee Williams

Success and failure are equally disastrous.
Tennessee Williams

Sometimes you can do all the right things and not
succeed. And that's a hard lesson of reality.
Donna Tartt

Dear Mrs. Wasson, who has remained
completely unspoiled by my success.
William Faulkner, inscription in book to Mrs. Ben Wasson

…an age and a time operating on the
premise that success is worth any price.
William Faulkner, letter to the *Memphis Commercial Appeal*

American culture is not just success, but generosity with success — a
culture of successful generosity. We desire and work to be successful in
order to be generous with the fruits of that success.
William Faulkner

What material success does is provide you with the ability to concentrate on other things that really matter. And that is being able to make a difference, not only in your own life, but in other people's lives.

Oprah Winfrey

THE SOUTH

Tell about the South. What it's like there. What they do there.
Why do they live there. Why do they live at all...
William Faulkner, *Absalom, Absalom*

The South has been pickled in the juice of its own image...
Barry Hannah, *Hey, Jack!*

Professional Southerners sicken me.
Barry Hannah

The Deep South might be wretched, but it can howl.
Barry Hannah

We lived from one great event to another tragic event, triumphant
events, with years of melancholy in between. We lost Vicksburg,
got slaughtered at Shiloh, fought duels, defied Huey
Long, and were bored to death between times.
Walker Percy, *Lancelot*

It's been said that Southern artists are a vanishing breed.
Where do you think we're going?
Glen Ray Tutor

I had an office in Washington, D.C., for 19 years, and I met
people who didn't know where their grandparents were
buried. In the South, that's just unheard of.
Governor Haley Barbour

Fincher was the kind of Southerner who will try to address you through
a web of deep and antic southernness, and who assumes everybody in
earshot knows all about his parents and history and wants to
hear an update about them at every opportunity.
Richard Ford, *The Sportswriter*

The South is the home of 'an eye for an eye.' Turning
the other cheek? The South can't see that.
Greg Iles

My ancestors fought for the Confederacy. I was raised in Natchez. I performed in the Confederate Pageant for a decade. I dug ditches and loaded truck with black men who taught me more than any book ever could. And I graduated from Ole Miss. Anyone who survived that is a de facto expert on the South.

Greg Iles

Through storytelling, the South reveals its soul.

Bill Ferris

Every southerner is not in the South.

Morgan Freeman

TALK

It's a human need. To talk about our lives.
It's an important human need.
Beth Henley, *Crimes of the Heart*

A lot of people believe what other people say.
B.B. King

People hear whispers as loud as guns.
Elizabeth Spencer, *The Voice at the Back Door*

To each other, they talked at a gallop. Literature turned them
on; their ideas flowed, ran back and forth like a current.
Elizabeth Spencer, *The Southern Woman: New and Selected Fiction*

With so much to say, the three said nothing.
John Grisham, *The Firm*

She get to yapping on the phone a million miles an hour.
Kathryn Stockett, *The Help*

It just feels kind of good to talk about someone else's screwed-up life.
Kathryn Stockett, *The Help*

I don't care 'bout no peoples in California… All I care about
is what the folks in Jackson, Mississippi, got to say.
Kathryn Stockett, *The Help*

Communication is awful hard between people.
Tennessee Williams, *Cat on a Hot Tin Roof*

I wasn't particular keen on listening at him,
but he still wasn't ready to shut up.
Armis Hawkins, *The Grand Leader*

I have discovered that most people have no one to talk to, no
one, that is, who really wants to listen.
Walker Percy, *The Moviegoer*

I have a need of silence and of stars. Too much is said too loudly.
I am dazed. The silken sound of whirled infinity
is lost in voices shouting to be heard.
William Alexander Percy

Humans generally get out the gist of what they need to say right at the
beginning, then spend forever qualifying, contradicting, burnishing,
or taking important things back. You rarely miss anything
by cutting most people off after two sentences.
Richard Ford, *The Lay of the Land*

Southerners love a good tale. They are born reciters, great memory
retainers, diary keepers, letter exchangers… great talkers.
Eudora Welty

For he was not strong enough to receive the impact of
unfamiliar things without a little talk to break their fall.
Eudora Welty, *The Collected Stories*

When night came, I was put to bed, but I would stay awake to listen to
Mama and Aunt Emma talk. Oh, the local stories they could tell…
killings, escapes, postmen being robbed, wives running
away at night, and teachers whipping students.
Theora Hamblett

Does it qualify as hearing voices if the voice you hear is your own?
Kevin Sessums

If you can't insult yourself, then who can you insult?
Kevin Sessums

When I recall my life in Mississippi, what I hear are
the rich sounds of the voices that surrounded me.
Kevin Sessums, *Mississippi Sissy*

When I'm talking to a large audience, I imagine that
I'm talking to a single person.
Red Barber

TROUBLE

…I was in trouble again.
Neil White, *In the Sanctuary of Outcasts*

Getting in trouble is lots of fun so long as you don't get caught.
Danny Ray McKittrick

It begun to soak in my head then, I might be in trouble. Big time.
Armis Hawkins, *The Grand Leader*

Men simply coped with the realities of their
hearts when they built prisons.
Richard Wright

We assumed God would never be so unkind as to give us more than one
system failure at a time. On Apollo 13, we had seven system failure
indicators light up at once. Jim Lovell said, 'Houston, we have a
problem.' But it was far from just one problem…
Fred Haise, Apollo 13 astronaut

You never want to take a step you can't back out of.
Fred Haise, on working to resolve the cascading
problems encountered by the Apollo 13 crew

Lord, these folks put so much compression on working men like me.
Johnny Ray Strong

I wanted to address the issue before it addressed me.
Robert Khayat, *The Education of a Lifetime*

TRUTH

It's hard to remember the truth when
there's so much truth to remember.
Testimony during criminal trial in U. S.
District Court, Northern District of Mississippi

The novelist's theme… is to tell the truth —
to distill the truth out of a story.
Shelby Foote

People make a grievous error thinking that a list of facts is the truth.
Facts are just the bare bones out of which truth is made.
Shelby Foote

A fact is not a truth until you love it.
Shelby Foote

The novelist and the historian are seeking the same thing: the truth
— not a different truth; the same truth — only they reach it, or try to
reach it by different routes. Whether the event took place in a world
now gone to dust, preserved by documents and evaluated by
scholarship, or in the imagination, preserved by memory and distilled
by the creative process, they both want to tell us how it was.
Shelby Foote

Just look what happens to poets… Half the time they go mad. And you
know why I think that happens? Too much truth distilled to its
essence, all surrounding evidence ignored or discarded.
Steve Yarborough, *Safe from the Neighbors*

The truth was flowing in torrents now, and they wanted all of it.
John Grisham, *The Summons*

It wasn't the truth he was after. It was victory.
Paige Mitchell, *Wilderness of Monkeys*

…crucified by truth.
Barry Hannah, *Airships*, "Water Liars"

Do you think it could be true that in our heart of hearts, we always know what is going to happen to us?
Walker Percy, *Lancelot*

I am not interested in gossip, but I am interested in candor.
Turner Catledge, *My Life at the Times*

I want to explain everything truthfully, and at the same time, to be always right, always charming, always lovable, always beautiful. Is that too much to ask?
Ellen Douglas, *A Lifetime Burning*

The truth won't always set you free.
Larry Brown, *Dirty Work*

Blanche: I don't tell truth. I tell what ought to be truth.
Tennessee Williams, *A Streetcar Named Desire*

…opposite things are very often done in getting at the truth.
Eudora Welty, Essay "Looking at Short Stories"

I can't believe Aibileen wants to tell Miss Skeeter the truth.
Kathryn Stockett, *The Help*

Truth. It feels cool, like water washing over my sticky-hot body. Cooling a heat that's been burning me up all my life.
Kathryn Stockett, *The Help*

Sometimes, in order to tell the truth, a writer must lie a little.
Willie Morris

Who can face truth? Can you?
Tennessee Williams, *Cat on a Hot Tin Roof*

Maybe it's being alive that makes them lie, and being almost not alive makes me sort of accidentally truthful.
Tennesse Williams, *Cat on a Hot Tin Roof*

Being friends is telling each other the truth.
Tennessee Williams, *Cat on a Hot Tin Roof*

If you want to know the truth, don't listen to what people tell you.
Richard Ford, *Wildlife*

Sportswriting... there is much truth to it, as well as plenty of lies.
Richard Ford, *The Sportswriter*

Most people... just make something up that's
patently ridiculous instead of saying the truth.
Richard Ford, *The Sportswriter*

I do not think it's a good idea to want to know what people
are thinking... People never tell the truth anyway.
Richard Ford, *The Sportswriter*

Too much truth can be worse than death, and last longer.
Richard Ford, *The Sportswriter*

Everything someone assures me to be true might not be.
Richard Ford, *Canada*

It's odd, though, what makes you think about the truth. It's so
rarely involved in the events of your life... Its finer
points seem impossible to find among the facts.
Richard Ford

Silas felt flattened by the truth.
Tom Franklin, *Crooked Letter, Crooked Letter*

Truth is like the sun. You can shut it out
for a time, but I ain't goin' away.
Elvis Presley

It's much easier for me to make major life, multi-million
dollar decisions, than it is to decide on a carpet
for my front porch. That's the truth.
Oprah Winfrey

Never be afraid to raise your voice for honesty and truth and compassion, against injustice and lying and greed.
William Faulkner, address to University High School

…truth was not where you were standing when you looked at it, but was an unalterable quality or thing which could, and would, knock your brains out if you did not accept it, or at least respect it.
William Faulkner, address to English Club at UVA

If I, who have had freedom all my life in which to write truth exactly as I saw it, visited Russia now… would be a betrayal, not of the giants: nothing can harm them, but of their spiritual heirs who risk their lives with every page they write… who have lost more than life: who have had their souls destroyed for the privilege of writing in public.
William Faulkner, letter to U.S. State Dept.

…the essential truth of these people and their doings, is the thing; the facts are not too important.
William Faulkner, letter to Albert Erskine on the discrepancies in the Snopes Trilogy

I believe that 'fact' has almost no connection with 'truth'…
William Faulkner, letter to Albert Erskine

…striving to capture, and thus fix for a moment on some pages, the truth of man's hope amidst the complexities of his heart.
William Faulkner, remarks on being presented the Venezuelan Order of Andrés Bello

What he sought and found and tried to capture was truth.
William Faulkner, remarks on receiving the Order of Andrés Bello

…anything in this manuscript that is true will be dull, and what is not dull probably won't be true.
William Faulkner, letter to Albert Erskine

The thing you fear most has no power. Your fear of it is what has the power. Facing the truth really will set you free.
Oprah Winfrey

Many Mississippians seem to love a good story more than the truth.
Claiborne Barksdale

He's always told lies… Perhaps he is not impressed with the truth.
Rick Bass, *Wild to the Heart*

…the basic human truth that the more you try to put something out of
your mind, the more difficult it becomes to think of anything else.
Greg Iles, *Natchez Burning*

Sometimes you studied a thing so hard for hidden significance
that you missed the neon-lit truth staring you in the face.
Greg Iles, *Natchez Burning*

The truth isn't hard to find if you're willing to get your
hands dirty. Truth waits just under the surface for any
man brave enough to scrape a little dirt away.
Greg Iles, *The Bone Tree*

People make a grievous error thinking that a list of facts is the truth.
Facts are just the bare bones out of which truth is made.
Greg Iles, *Natchez Burning*

We judge and punish based on facts, but facts are not truth. Facts are
like a buried skeleton uncovered long after death. Truth is fluid. Truth
is alive. To know the truth requires understanding, the most difficult
human art. It requires seeing all things at once, forward
and backward, the way God sees.
Greg Iles, *Dead Sleep*

If a man is forced to choose between the truth and
his father, only a fool chooses the truth.
Greg Iles, *Natchez Burning*

…the only truths that matter to me are the
ones I don't, and can't, understand.
Donna Tartt, *The Goldfinch*

We can't choose what we want and don't want and that's the hard, lonely truth. Sometimes we want what we want, even if we know it's going to kill us. We can't escape who we are.
Donna Tartt, *The Goldfinch*

It's true… I saw it. It was on television.
Donna Tartt, *The Secret History*

And as much as I'd like to believe there's a truth beyond illusion, I've come to believe that there's no truth beyond illusion.
Donna Tartt, *The Goldfinch*

Art is never the voice of a country; it is an even more precious thing, the voice of the individual, doing its best to speak, not comfort of any sort, but truth.
Eudora Welty

It takes a mentor to direct the aimless and offer them difficult truths meant to challenge, not bruise.
Ronnie Agnew

…every page was a battle with myself because I knew I had to tell the truth. That's what the memoir form demands.
Jesmyn Ward

In life, finding a voice is speaking and living the truth.
John Grisham

VICKSBURG

I will move upon Vicksburg and will take it.
General Ulysses S. Grant

The Battle of Vicksburg... resembled a messy chess game,
filled with unpleasant and dangerous surprises amid
the ruthless grind to capture the rebel king.
Winston Groom, Vicksburg 1863

Vicksburg, the bluff top river town was his goal.
Shelby Foote, on General Ulysses S. Grant, *The Beleaguered City*

The road to the White House led through Vicksburg.
Shelby Foote, *The Beleaguered City*

You have command of all troops sent to your department,
and have permission to fight the enemy where you please.
Message from General-in-Chief Henry Halleck to
General Ulysses S. Grant regarding Vicksburg

Grant considered himself unleashed.
Shelby Foote, *The Beleaguered City*

With Halleck's telegram... Grant felt secure
from possible thunder from on high.
Shelby Foote, *The Beleaguered City*

Two commanders on the same field are always one too many.
General Ulysses S. Grant, on the contest between himself and
General McClernand over command of the Vicksburg operation

The opening of the Mississippi River will be to us of more
advantage than the capture of forty Richmonds.
General-in-Chief Henry Halleck to General Ulysses S. Grant

We must not fail in this if within human power to accomplish it.
General-in-Chief Henry Halleck to General Ulysses S. Grant on Vicksburg

Go ahead fast.
Admiral Porter to his ironclad during Vicksburg campaign

Grant will fail miserably, hopelessly, eternally.
Murat Halstead on General Ulysses S. Grant at Vicksburg

I think Grant has hardly a friend left, except myself.
President Abraham Lincoln on General Ulysses S. Grant

If I knew what brand of whiskey he drinks, I would
send a barrel or so to some other generals.
President Abraham Lincoln on General Ulysses S. Grant

A man who could be silent in several languages.
Shelby Foote, comment on Grant, *The Beleaguered City*

There was no nonsense, no sentiment; only there for the one
single purpose of getting that command over the
river in the shortest time possible.
Shelby Foote, comment on General Ulysses S. Grant in Vicksburg Campaign

The roads... were little more than trails of slime through
the surrounding ooze, not quite firm enough for
wagons, nor quite wet enough for boats.
Shelby Foote, *The Beleaguered City*

I reached Vicksburg at the time appointed,
landed, assaulted, and failed.
General William Tecumseh Sherman, on his
defeat at Chickasaw Bayou, three miles north of Vicksburg

Vicksburg is the strongest place I ever saw... No place on earth is
favored by nature with natural defenses as is Vicksburg.
General William Tecumseh Sherman

Vicksburg should have ended the war, but the rebel leaders were mad.
General William Tecumpseh Sherman

Resting in Vicksburg seemed like resting near a volcano.
Mary Ann Loughborough, resident of Vicksburg during the siege

I stand on ground once hollowed by a web of caves…
what is to become of all the living things in this place?
Natasha Trethewey, "Pilgrimage"

The Father of Waters again goes unvexed to the sea.
President Abraham Lincoln, on the fall of Vicksburg

When the last pound of beef, bacon, and flour, the last grain of corn,
the last cow and hog and horse and dog shall have been
consumed, and the last man shall have perished in the
trenches, then and only then will I sell Vicksburg.
Confederate General John Pemberton

The fate of the Confederacy was sealed at Vicksburg.
General Ulysses S. Grant

VIOLENCE

It takes the midnight mind to do the black deed to the black man.
Elizabeth Spencer, *The Voice at the Back Door*

Eleven years old and already knife-cut in a whorehouse brawl.
William Faulkner, *The Reivers*

Folks don't start lynching in daylight… they don't start them by
daylight because then they would have to see one another's faces.
William Faulkner, *Intruder in the Dust*

I was the sort that tended to bear grudges. I didn't like
anybody correcting me on anything, for any reason.
Barry Hannah, *Geronimo Rex*

That was the kind of wrath you didn't mess with.
Barry Hannah, *Geronimo Rex*

…walking along in the filthy reality of the metropolis (New York) as bait
for the muggers… who knows what marvels of violence would ensue.
Barry Hannah, *The Tennis Handsome*

It was an honorable and violent family… The great-grandfather knew
what was what and said so and acted accordingly and did not care what
anyone thought. He… once met the Grand Wizard of the
Ku Klux Klan in a barbershop and invited him then
and there to shoot it out in the street.
Walker Percy, *The Last Gentleman*

Stanley's always smashed things.
Tennessee Williams, *A Streetcar Named Desire*

Mississippians earned less, killed more,
and died younger than other Americans.
David Oshinsky, *Worse than Slavery*

In 1905, Joshua Ridgeway was shot and killed in a barroom brawl in front of the old Hotel Greenville. Mr. Ridgeway died in a vicious gunfight, in which he killed two other gentlemen. For his tombstone, the family selected, "Blessed are the peacemakers."
Gayden Metcalfe, *Being Dead is No Excuse*

These were the rhythms of his life: indifference and violence.
Richard Wright, *Native Son*

Code One — cross burning
Code Two — whipping
Code Three — arson
Code Four — death
Ku Klux Klan codes for violent action

I just meant to shoot the motherfucker in the head and two times in the chest. Him dying was between him and the Lord.
Bluesman R.L. Burnside

The first thing you want to do after being shot is make sure you are not shot again.
Ace Atkins

There is nothing less invigorating than to be shot at with result.
David Crews (Apologies to Winston Churchill)

…how can you possible justify cold-blooded murder? Henry lit a cigarette. 'I prefer to think of it,' he said, 'as redistribution of matter.'
Donna Tartt, *The Secret History*

…Katrina, the mother that swept into the Gulf and slaughtered. Her chariot was a storm so great and black, the Greeks would say it was harnessed to dragons.
Jesmyn Ward, *Salvage the Bones*

Katrina is the mother we will remember until the next mother with large, merciless hands, committed to blood, comes.
Jesmyn Ward, *Salvage the Bones*

Mississippians have been shooting and killing each other…to a greater extent than in all the other states of the Union put together.

Emissary to President Andrew Johnson

What I especially liked about Geronimo then was that he had cheated, lied, stolen, mutinied, usurped, killed, burned, raped, pillaged, razed, trapped, ripped, mashed, bowshot, stomped, herded, exploded, cut, stoned, revenged, prevenged, avenged, and was his own man.

Barry Hannah, *Geronimo Rex*

VIRTUE

Virtue…cold and odorless and tasteless virtue.
William Faulkner, *The Reivers*

Someday we'll run out of angles and get back to virtues.
William Faulkner

It is sophistry to speak of two sets of virtues; there is but one: virtue is
an end in itself; the survival virtues are means, not ends. Honor and
honesty, compassion and truth are good even if they kill
you, for they alone give life its dignity and worth.
William Alexander Percy, *Lanterns on the Levee*

We will not be saved by our virtues, but by our demographics.
Ralph Eubanks

WAR

…war meant widows' tears and orphans' howls.
Shelby Foote, *Shiloh*

War? One can lose oneself in the joy of battle, in fighting
for a glorious cause, but there are not many
glorious causes for which to fight these days.
Donna Tartt, *The Secret History*

War is a species of passionate insanity.
Mary Ann Loughborough of Vicksburg

War... you would not miss it for anything. It is your war…
Something that big going on in the world and be
nineteen years old and miss it? It's unbelievable.
Shelby Foote, on World War II

Hitler went into Poland; I protested by going
into the Mississippi National Guard.
Shelby Foote

It sounded suspiciously easy.
Hodding Carter, on his World War II military orders

If there was an army regulation they didn't violate,
it was because they hadn't heard of it.
Hodding Carter, *Where Main Street Meets the River*

There was almost a full day's work in each week.
Hodding Carter, on his service in the Pentagon

Lieutenant Waverly Wray was a big man, 250 pounds with legs like tree
trunks. The standard-issue Army parachute wasn't large enough for his
weight, and he dropped too fast on his jumps, but the men
said, 'Hell, with his legs, he don't need a chute.'
Stephen Ambrose, *Citizen Soldiers* (Waverly Wray was from
Panola County, Mississippi)

Wray was as experienced and skilled as an
infantry soldier can get and still be alive.
Colonel Ben Vandervoort, quoted in *Citizen Soldier*

Who's got more grenades?
Lieutenant Waverly Wray in Normandy on June 7, 1944, immediately following an
engagement in which he singlehandedly killed 10 German soldiers, while he
suffered a bullet wound which tore off half of his right ear

**Colonel Ben Vandervoort to a wounded Lieutenant
Waverly Wray**: They've been getting kind of close to
you, haven't they Waverly?
Lieutenant Waverly Wray: Not as close as I've been getting
to them, sir.

In the army, you slept in a barracks with all kinds of people of
every nationality, every trade, every character and quality
you can imagine, and that was a good experience.
Shelby Foote

Grant was something rare in war. He could learn from experience.
Shelby Foote

A rich man's war and a poor man's fight…
Shelby Foote

Who else could have declared a war…except men who would believe
that all necessary to conduct a successful war was not acumen nor
shrewdness nor politics or diplomacy nor money nor even integrity and
simple arithmetic but just love of land and courage.
William Faulkner, *Go Down Moses*

WEATHER

A Mississippi summer is an awesome and boggling thing, a slab
of steaming time a hundred cubed: a hundred days at a
hundred degrees and a hundred percent humidity.
Jack Butler, *Jujitsu for Christ*

August in Mississippi is different from July. As to heat, it is not
a question of degree but of kind. July heat is furious, but in
August, the heat has killed even itself and lies dead over us.
Elizabeth Spencer, *Fire in the Morning*

The humidity factor has never, to my knowledge, been taken into
account in descriptions of Hell. You talking eternal fire
without no humidity, a Mississippian is gonna think
you mean Heaven or Southern California.
Jack Butler, *Jujitsu for Christ*

Up home we loved a good storm coming; we'd fly outdoors and run up
and down to meet it… The wilder it blew, the better we liked it.
Eudora Welty, *The Optimist's Daughter*

Don't let the weather bluff you — bluff the weather.
William Faulkner

…a dozen different weathers can happen in 30 minutes.
William Faulkner

The traditional Southern holiday weather of gray skies and cold rain.
John Grisham, *The Firm*

It should rain at funerals.
Paige Mitchell, *A Wilderness of Monkeys*

It was hot as a fresh-fucked fox in a forest fire.
Larry Brown, *Dirty Work*

A summer month could stretch on for years.
Kathryn Stockett, *The Help*

I sweat like iced tea in August.
Kathryn Stockett, *The Help*

Minny don't stop sweating for five minutes in
January, and maybe not even then.
Kathryn Stockett, *The Help*

Mississippi got the most unorganized weather in the nation.
Kathryn Stockett, *The Help*

…ice so thick it would take a hundred Mississippi summers to melt it.
Kathryn Stockett, *The Help*

A semitropical country of blast furnace summers
and fire and brimstone religion.
William Doyle's description of Mississippi, *American Insurrection*

A mere Virginian cannot be expected to cope with such heat. You've
got to walk through it gently, don't make any superfluous moves.
Shelby Foote to William Styron at William Faulkner's funeral

The murderous eye of the sun.
Larry Brown, *Father and Son*

Our greatest worry is the weather — as the
weather goes, so goes Mississippi's year.
Mississippi WPA Guide

WOMEN

I had learned… how to approach language, words… with a kind of
alert respect, as you approach dynamite; even with joy as you approach
women; perhaps with the same secretly unscrupulous intentions.
William Faulkner

Every small town needs one like me. A spicy, old spinster
that goes around meddlin' in other people's business.
Paige Mitchell, *Wilderness of Monkeys*

These old guitars are just like women: when you get 'em
out in public, you never know what they're going to do.
Son House

Blanche: Oh, in my youth I excited some admiration.
Tennessee Williams, *A Streetcar Named Desire*

Honey, you'd sooner get a certified letter from
Satan as to mess with me tonight.
Bill Dunlap, *Short Mean Fiction*

I'm leaving you, mean Mama
Just to worry you off my mind.
Jimmie Rodgers, "Jimmie's Mean Mama Blues"

But why should I cast myself in the ancient female
part of victim of men's plots and passions?
Ellen Douglas, *A Lifetime Burning*

…the women, the indomitable, the undefeated, who never
surrendered… who… would get up and walk out of *Gone With the Wind*
as soon as Sherman's name was mentioned; irreconcilable and enraged
and still talking about it (the Civil War) long after the weary
exhausted men who had fought and lost it gave up
trying to make them hush.
William Faulkner, *Essay on Mississippi*

Babe, why did you shoot Zachery?
'Cause I didn't like his looks. I just didn't like his looks.
Beth Henley, *Crimes of the Heart*

Babe: I wonder… why Mama hung herself.
Meg: She had a bad day. A real bad day.
Beth Henley, *Crimes of the Heart*

Lenny: I told him we should never see each other again.
Meg: Well, if you told him, you can just untell him.
Beth Henley, *Crimes of the Heart*

I've had just about my full of you trashy McGraths and your
trashy ways: hanging yourselves in cellars; carrying on
with married men; shooting your own husbands!
Beth Henley, *Crimes of the Heart*

Girls who had been pretty so long, they looked tired of it.
Barry Hannah, *Geronimo Rex*

Levaster's mother came too, talking about the weather and
her new shoes. Someone mistook her for nothing
in one of the chairs and sat on her.
Barry Hannah, *The Tennis Handsome*

I spend the entire time working, making money, going to
movies, and seeking the company of women.
Walker Percy, *The Moviegoer*

I shall never understand women.
Walker Percy, *Lancelot*

Her not being here was like oxygen not being here.
Walker Percy, *Lancelot*

…I make one of the biggest discoveries of my life… It is this: there is
life to be lived… and most of all… no: all of all: a woman to love.
Walker Percy, *Lancelot*

Blanche: Stella, oh Stella, Stella! Stella for Star!
Tennessee Williams, *A Streetcar Named Desire*

Blanche: I understand there's to be a little card party to which we ladies are cordially not invited!
Tennessee Williams, *A Streetcar Named Desire*

Blanche: Clothes are my passion!
Tennessee Williams, *A Streetcar Named Desire*

Stanley: I never met a woman that didn't know if she was good-looking or not without being told…
Tennessee Williams, *A Streetcar Named Desire*

Stanley: STELL-LAHHHHHHH!
Tennessee Williams, *A Streetcar Named Desire*

Blanche: A single girl… has got to keep a firm hold on her emotions or she'll be lost!
Tennessee Williams, *A Streetcar Named Desire*

Blanche: I have always depended on the kindness of strangers.
Tennessee Williams, *A Streetcar Named Desire*

Why's she wearing all that goo on her face? I'll bet she's got on double the makeup the other white ladies wear.
Kathryn Stockett, *The Help*

She's almost as big as me, except she's skinny in all those places I ain't.
Kathryn Stockett, *The Help*

Don't you ever let that white lady find you sitting on her toilet. I don't care if you've got to go so bad it's coming out of your hairbraids.
Kathryn Stockett, *The Help*

Miss Celia comes in the kitchen… She's wearing a tight red sweater and a red skirt and enough makeup to scare a hooker.
Kathryn Stockett, *The Help*

Miss Myrna's gone shit-house crazy on us,
drunk hair spray or something.
Kathryn Stockett, *The Help*

Some dormant instinct tells me to smile, run my hand
through my hair. I feel ridiculous, but I do it.
Kathryn Stockett, *The Help*

Hilly was tanning in the sun. I was fanning in the murky shade.
Kathryn Stockett, *The Help*

Lord, that girl's hot as Tunica blacktop.
Kathryn Stockett, *The Help*

The room is full of cake-eating, Tab-drinking,
cigarette-smoking women.
Kathryn Stockett, *The Help*

Do you still live at home?
Yes, I still live at home.
...for God's sake, you're a twenty-four-year-old educated
woman. Go get an apartment.
Kathryn Stockett, *The Help*

I've been kicked out of the bridge club... I don't get invited to cocktail
parties or baby showers anymore... I tell myself, 'That's what you get
when you put thirty-one toilets on the most popular girl's front yard.'
People tend to treat you a little differently than before.
Kathryn Stockett, *The Help*

Gertrude is every Southern white woman's nightmare. I adore her.
Kathryn Stockett, *The Help*

I wait on white ladies who walk right out the bedroom
wearing nothing but they personality.
Kathryn Stockett, *The Help*

Minny is Minny, all the time.
Kathryn Stockett, *The Help*

As usual, Minny's house be like a chicken coop on fire. Minny be hollering; things be flinging around, all the kids squawking.
Kathryn Stockett, *The Help*

Hating Miss Hilly's the only thing that crazy woman and I have in common.
Kathryn Stockett, *The Help*

The worst reconciliation with a woman is better than the best one you work out with yourself.
Richard Ford, *The Sportswriter*

Ladies from the altar guild (at St. James Episcopal in Greenville) have been known to visit the Vatican only to sniff, 'That's not how it's done at St. James.'
Gayden Metcalfe, *Being Dead Is No Excuse*

You can't be too thin or have too much silver.
Gayden Metcalfe, *Being Dead Is No Excuse*

I can't go to parties and date boys and take all these hard courses. I have to make a choice.
Gayden Meltcalfe, *Being Dead Is No Excuse*, Olivia Morgan on why she dropped out of school

Going outside the house without a hat and gloves is one step away from going to the Starketa Grocery naked.
Gayden Metcalfe, *Being Dead Is No Excuse*

It'll be the first time Aunt Weezy and I ever got within ten feet of each other without her telling me to stand up straight and brush the hair out of my eyes.
Gayden Metcalfe, *Being Dead Is No Excuse*

Mrs. Lowrey may have been a better general than General Lowrey. While the general was off at war with colonels and captains to support him, Mrs. Lowrey raised, educated, clothed, and fed an army of 11 children by herself, made a crop, and kept the family together.
History of General Mark Perrin Lowrey

Bacall looks at Bogart to light her cigarette. Bogart looks at
her for a minute, sizes her up, then tosses her the
matches for her to light her own cigarette.
William Faulkner's description of a scene for *To Have and Have Not*

I've been your gentleman friend for quite a while now.
Ain't it time I was promoted?
William Faulkner to actress Ruth Ford

Women are tougher than evil.
William Faulkner

It's not men who cope with death; they resist, try to fight back, and get
their brains trampled out in consequence; where women just
flank it, envelop it in one soft and instantaneous
confederation of unresistance…
William Faulkner, *The Reivers*

…women are wonderful. They can bear anything because they are wise
enough to know that all you have to do with grief and trouble is just go
on through them and come out on the other side. I think they can do
this because they not only decline to dignify physical pain by taking it
seriously, they have no sense of shame at the idea of being knocked out.
William Faulkner, *The Reivers*

When someone asked me why he (Faulkner) disliked women so.
I said that I wasn't aware that he did. I was scared
he liked women a little too much.
Estelle Faulkner

I seem to know — I am coming to believe — so little about all women.
William Faulkner in a letter to Joan Williams

To Pat, who is always good to me whether I've
been thrown over by a horse or a dame.
William Faulkner, thank you note to Pat Klopfer

It's silly to talk about women as if they were dishonest men.
They're not like men at all; they're just women.
William Faulkner in a conversation with Joseph Blotner

She's something of the new age, wiggling even while she's standing still.
William Faulkner, on Marilyn Monroe

Women are just born with a practical fertility of suspicion...
William Faulkner

I am a woman in process. I'm just trying like everybody
else. I try to take every conflict, every experience,
and learn from it. Life is never dull.
Oprah Winfrey

Biology is the least of what makes someone a mother.
Oprah Winfrey

I'm not even kind of a lesbian.
Oprah Winfrey

A man's got to do what a man's got to do.
A woman must do what he can't.
Barry Hannah

Sometimes it's hard to be a woman, giving all your love to just one man.
Tammy Wynette

I'm not going to be some Tammy Wynette,
stand-by-your-man, little woman.
Hillary Clinton

Why would I want female friends? They can't talk about football,
or duck hunting, or politics, or lawsuits, or anything that I
want to talk about. They talk about kids, clothes, recipes,
coupons, furniture, stuff I know nothing about.
John Grisham, *A Time to Kill*

Abby... dreamed of babies. Mitch thought they
were cute, but was not inspired.
John Grisham, *The Firm*

She… spent all of her adult life seeking social advancement
in a town where there was none to be had.

John Grisham, *The Firm*

He admired her legs, which… were positioned
just so and demanded to be admired.

John Grisham, *The Firm*

Kudzu sallies into the gully
like a man pulling up a chair
where a woman was happily dining alone.

Beth Ann Fennelly, *The Kudzu Chronicles*

He didn't know what women expected you to do anyway. Work like a
dog forty hours a week, stay home on Saturday night, go to church
on Sunday, and give them all your money, he guessed.

Larry Brown, *Father and Son*

That woman can sell water to a drowning man.

Donna Tartt, *The Goldfinch*

I missed her so much I wanted to die; a hard, physical
longing, like a craving for air underwater.

Donna Tartt, *The Goldfinch*

She was a living reverie for me: the mere sight of her sparked an almost
infinite range of fantasy, from Greek to Gothic, from vulgar to divine.

Donna Tartt, *The Secret History*

Try to avoid getting involved with somebody who's gonna
need killing before it's over. It may seem to you that
narrows the field somewhat, but be diligent.

Jill Connor Browne, *The Sweet Potato Queens Book of Love*

Cheap jewelry is worse than no jewelry at all, and there are very
few things in life that are worse than no jewelry at all.

Jill Connor Browne, *The Sweet Potato Queens Book of Love*

There is nothing so thrilling as a woman of words when
she decides that the time for words is past.

Greg Iles, *The Footprints of God*

Don't keep a girl guessing too long, or she'll
find the answer somewhere else.

Greg Iles, *Natchez Burning*

Like my best friend, I asked for drums for Christmas. But when he
moved on to guitar, I realized two things: first, guitar is a much more
expressive instrument, and second, way more girls pay
attention to guitar players than to drummers.

Greg Iles

Nothing in the world is as hopeful as knowing a woman you like is
somewhere thinking about only you. Conversely, there is
no badness anywhere as acute as the badness of no
woman out in the world thinking about you.

Richard Ford, *The Sportswriter*

WRITING

There are people in history who epitomize what an artist should be...
Shakespeare is an obvious example. Beethoven is another.
Faulkner is that kind of writing figure.

Shelby Foote

Literature is the history of the soul.

Barry Hannah

It is so hard to write. So hard to finish, so hard to
find the exact word to make it shine.

Ellen Gilchrist, *The Writing Life*

Don't overwrite description in a story — you haven't got time.

Elizabeth Spencer

People who love books sooner or later dream of writing
them. It's a natural response to stimuli.

Ellen Gilchrist, *The Writing Life*

The way you start writing is by writing.

Ellen Gilchrist, *The Writing Life*

We live at the level of our language. Whatever we can articulate,
we can imagine or understand or explore.

Ellen Gilchrist, *Falling Through Space*

I'm impatient with writers who make too much sense.

Barry Hannah

Faulkner didn't exaggerate in his stories.
He toned them down, if anything.

Phil Stone

The artist doesn't have time to listen to critics. The ones who
want to be writers read the reviews, the ones who want to
write don't have time to read the reviews.

William Faulkner

My trouble as a poet is that I keep one eye on the
ball and the other eye on Babe Ruth.
William Faulkner

I learned from Hemingway that roughness should
be part of the smoothness…
Shelby Foote

I'm not talking about making it livelier than it was, I'm just talking
about some attempt to make it as lively as it was.
Shelby Foote, on writing history

Writing, to him, was what living was all about.
Shelby Foote, on Faulkner

When I write about a battle… I look at the
foliage, smell the land, watch the sky.
Shelby Foote

I am crazy about words, and I am crazy about compression.
Shelby Foote, on writing

I am never inclined to take very seriously the judgements of literary
coteries. I think they can be depended upon to miss the point.
Shelby Foote

Writing is tough… But it is supposed to be tough.
Shelby Foote

Style is not… flourishes. Style is the way a man is able
to communicate to you the quality of his mind.
Shelby Foote

Wolfe is a writer for young people… he won't do in the
long run, which is the only run that counts.
Shelby Foote

I happen to believe that the worst place on God's earth
for a creative writer is a college campus.
Shelby Foote

The silences are sometimes more important than the action.
Shelby Foote

I've always been glad that I enjoyed dances and helling around the
Delta. It's where I got much of the material I use…
Shelby Foote

The real answers, the answers that will bring you not peace
but understanding, can only be found in art.
Shelby Foote

I always discourage young writers. Those who are destined to
write won't listen to me, and those who aren't might.
Shelby Foote

To really know a thing, you've got to feel it on your skin.
Shelby Foote

(Faulkner's book) was good, even though a few readers complained
that they never before had read thirty thousand
words divided into only three sentences.
Hodding Carter, *Where Main Street Meets the River*

He aspired only to writing good novels… and
remaining a chronic buck private.
Hodding Carter, *Where Main Street Meets the River*, on Irwin Shaw

What I have tried to do in my writing is to show my fellow
Southerners what is still wrong about us and tell our fellow
Americans elsewhere what is right about us.
Hodding Carter, *Where Main Street Meets the River*

We have talked much about writers and writing… and about how
it is sometimes possible to eat regularly from its practice.
Herschel Brickell

Whitman described writing, like love, as 'sweet Hell'… My hope is that
this book may help those who read it move a little closer
to the sweet and a little farther from the Hell.
Herschel Brickell

I'd written it (a poem) in a gust of all the culture I had in me.
Barry Hannah, *Geronimo Rex*

I am writing this because I don't owe myself anything except writing.
Barry Hannah, *Captain Maximus*

Nothing is sacred; I tell everything.
Barry Hannah, *Hey, Jack!*

…I love the English language very much… I just adore it.
Barry Hannah

If I hadn't had it (tuberculosis) I might be a second-rate
shrink practicing in Birmingham, at best.
Walker Percy

If it hadn't been for Uncle Will, I probably
would have ended up a car dealer.
Walker Percy, on William Alexander Percy

He was the fabled relative, the one you like to speculate about… the
fact that he was a lawyer and a planter didn't cut much ice — after all,
the South was full of lawyer-planters. But how many people did
you know who were war heroes and wrote books of poetry?
Walker Percy, on William Alexander Percy

I would hurl words into the darkness and wait for an echo.
If an echo sounded, no matter how faintly, I would
send other words to tell, to march, to fight.
Richard Wright, *American Hunger*

The burning drive of the young, the desire to live, to do, to make, to
achieve, no matter what the sacrifice, is the feeling most
surpassingly alive to the author, most moving to us.
Eudora Welty, Essay, "The House of Willa Cather"

Faulkner's prose… is intolerantly and intolerably
unanalyzable and quite pure…
Eudora Welty, review of William Faulkner's *Intruder in the Dust*

Promoters of products, promoters of causes, promoters of self, have a
common language, though one with a small vocabulary.

Eudora Welty, review of S.J. Perleman's *Baby, It's Cold Outside*

One way of looking at Moby Dick is that his task as a symbol
was so big and strenuous that he had to be a whale.

Eudora Welty, *Words into Fiction*

Bring us one of your stories. Don't bother to
read it. Just tell it in your own words.

Letter to Eudora Welty from women's club that asked her to speak to their club

It's living that makes me want to write.

Eudora Welty

Life, whatever its problems, always bears gifts, and
one of Mississippi's great fruits is our writers.

Richard Howorth

The only way you're going to keep sharp is to read and write every day.

Kathryn Stockett, *The Help*

I sat in the study parlor and wrote for hours — mostly term papers but
also short stories, bad poetry, episodes of *Dr. Kildare*, Pall Mall jingles,
letters of complaint, ransom notes, love letters to boys I'd seen in class
but hadn't had the nerve to speak to, all of which I never mailed.

Kathryn Stockett, *The Help*

…my dream was that one day I would write something
that people would actually read.

Kathryn Stockett, *The Help*

You will never meet anybody sitting at that typewriter.

Kathryn Stockett, *The Help*

The artist must bow to the monster of his own imagination.

Richard Wright

A writer's life is, at best, bizarre, and, at worst, horrendous.

Willie Morris, foreword to *The Last of the Southern Girls*

There were two Willies: the one who wrote a life and the
one who lived a life, and… there's a good chance
neither would have recognized the other.

Larry L. King, *In Search of Willie Morris*

Luxury is the wolf at the door, and its fangs are the
vanities and conceits germinated by success. When an
artist learns this, he knows where the danger is.

Tennessee Williams

What are artists? Desperate searchers after whatever can be found of
truth and beauty, even when the two may be poles apart.

Tennessee Williams

There's the facts. Wrote them there myself.

Servetus Crockett Barr, Mississippi store owner

For writers… bad news is always easier than
good, since it is, after all, more familiar.

Richard Ford, *The Sportswriter*

When asked by the local newspaper if I wanted to be a
local correspondent I said, 'Well I've never written anything.
Why would you come to me?' As it turned out the local librarian told
the editor I read more books than anybody else in town, and
since I read so much, maybe I could write.

Lucy Morgan of Hattiesburg, Mississippi, a Pulitzer Prize-winning
journalist with the *St. Pete Times* in Florida

All good art is an indiscretion.

Tennessee Williams

If the writing is honest, it cannot be
separated from the man who wrote it.

Tennessee Williams

Why did I write? Because I found life unsatisfactory.

Tennessee Williams

I'm only really alive when I'm writing.
Tennessee Williams

I have always been pushed by the negative. The apparent failure
of a play sends me back to my typewriter that very night,
before the reviews are out. I am more compelled
to get back to work than if I had a success.
Tennessee Williams

I have a theory… that someplace at the heart of most
compelling stories is something that doesn't make sense.
Richard Ford

Things would get in my brain that I couldn't get out of my brain.
Richard Ford

I don't have a very logical and orderly mind.
Richard Ford

Happiness, for me, is getting to write about
the most important things I know.
Richard Ford

I work really hard at these books, and when colleagues write
nasty reviews of them, I take it very personally.
Richard Ford

Reading is probably what leads most writers to writing.
Richard Ford

In order to write novels for a living, I do think and worry and
brood and fidget about stuff that I'm working on.
Richard Ford

Maybe I'm a serial regional writer. First
here, then there, across the map.
Richard Ford

Writing never came naturally, and I still have to force my hand to do it.
Richard Ford

The ways in which things are superficially similar,
but also distinct, is interesting to me.
Richard Ford

I've muddled through a lot of things, but I have not muddled through
my writing life. I work absolutely flat out, giving it my all.
Richard Ford

I decided early on that I wanted to participate in the greater
American experience, rather than the parochial one in Mississippi.
But I have an urge as a writer to meld the Southern
experience into the larger American one.
Richard Ford

Literature has as one of its principal allures that it tells
you something about life that life itself can't tell you.
Richard Ford

I believe in the ideas of 'normal' in the way that I believe
in the idea of logic, or the idea of character. All of these
ethical constructs are just that: constructs.
Richard Ford

It is no loss to mankind when one writer decides to call it a day.
When a tree falls in the forest, who cares but the monkeys?
Richard Ford, *The Sportswriter*

You can only write a good story or a good novel by yourself.
Richard Ford

...for real writers, unfortunately, their club is a club of just one member.
Richard Ford, *The Sportswriter*

The job of the writer is to change the way the reader sees the world.
Richard Ford

With imagination, you can put something where nothing was.
Richard Ford

Find what causes a commotion in your heart.
Find a way to write about that.
Richard Ford

If you want to study writing, read Dickens. That's how to study
writing — or Faulkner or D.H. Lawrence or John Keats. They
can teach you everything you need to know about writing.
Shelby Foote

I'm a slow writer: five, six hundred words is a good day.
That's the reason it took me 20 years to write those
million and a half words of the Civil War.
Shelby Foote

Everything you do helps you to write if you're a writer. Adversity and
success both contribute largely to making you what you are.
Shelby Foote

I've never shown anybody a draft of anything.
Shelby Foote

Most of my inspiration, if that's the word, came from books themselves.
Shelby Foote

I don't want anything to do with anything mechanical between me and
the paper, including a typewriter, and I don't even want a
fountain pen between me and the paper.
Shelby Foote

I began the way nearly everybody I ever heard of. I
began writing poetry. And I find that to be quite usual
with writers, trying their hand at poetry.
Shelby Foote

I thought I needed booze to write. I'm glad I was disabused.
Barry Hannah

I found out about reviews early on. They're mostly written by sad men
on bad afternoons. That's probably why I'm less angry than some
writers, who are so narcissistic they consider every line of every
review, even a thoughtful one, as major treason.
Barry Hannah

I'll tell you why I like writing: it's just jumping into a pool. I get myself into a kind of trance. I engage the world, but it's also wonderful to just escape. I try to find the purities out of the confusion.
Barry Hannah

I was always kind of florid and full of rhetoric. That was my flaw.
Barry Hannah

I don't write under the ghost of Faulkner. I live in the same town and find his life and work inspiring, but that's it. I have a motorcycle and tool along the country lanes. I travel at my own speed.
Barry Hannah

All serious daring starts from within.
Eudora Welty

Greater than scene is situation. Greater than situation is implication. Greater than all of these is a single, entire human being, who will never be confined in any frame.
Eudora Welty

To imagine yourself inside another person… is what a storywriter does in every piece of work; it is his first step, and his last too, I suppose.
Eudora Welty

The events in our lives happen in a sequence in time, but in their significance to ourselves, they find their own order the continuous thread of revelation.
Eudora Welty

Writing fiction has developed in me an abiding respect for the unknown in a human lifetime and a sense of where to look for the threads, how to follow, how to connect, find in the thick of the tangle what clear line persists.
Eudora Welty
Writers and travelers are mesmerized alike by knowing of their destinations.
Eudora Welty

Writing a story or a novel is one way of discovering sequence in experience, of stumbling upon cause and effect in the happenings of a writer's own life.
Eudora Welty

It had been startling and disappointing to me to find out that story books had been written by people, that books were not natural wonders, coming of themselves like grass.
Eudora Welty

There is absolutely everything in great fiction but a clear answer.
Eudora Welty

If you haven't surprised yourself, you haven't written.
Eudora Welty

She was sent to sleep under a velvety cloak of works, richly patterned and stitched with gold, straight out of a fairy tale, while they went reading on into her dreams.
Eudora Welty, *The Optimist's Daughter*

The novelist works neither to correct nor to condone, not at all to comfort, but to make what's told alive.
Eudora Welty, *On Writing*

The impulse to dream was slowly beaten out of me by experience. Now it surged up again, and I hungered for books, new ways of looking and seeing.
Richard Wright

Don't leave inferences to be drawn when evidence can be presented.
Richard Wright

Winston, don't change a word of it.
Willie Morris, after reading the first draft of Forrest Gump

It's a lot easier to throw a perfect pass than to write a perfect sentence.
Greg Iles

When I'm writing, I am concentrating almost wholly on concrete detail: the color a room is painted, the way a drop of water rolls off a well leaf after a rain.
Donna Tartt

I write all the time, like a pianist with scales or an artist with a sketchbook.
Donna Tartt

Donna Tartt is the kind of writer who makes other writers pea green with envy.
New York Times

Storytelling and elegant style don't always go hand in hand.
Donna Tartt

The storytelling gift is innate: one has it or one doesn't. But style is at least partly a learned thing: one refines it by looking and listening and reading and practice — by work.
Donna Tartt

Murder is a subject that has always drawn people for as long as people have been telling stories.
Donna Tartt

I'd rather write one good book than ten mediocre ones.
Donna Tartt

The job of the novelist is to invent: to embroider, to color, to embellish, to make things up.
Donna Tartt

Writing is a lonely business.
Donna Tartt

I love the tradition of Dickens, where even the most minor walk-on characters are twitching and particular and alive.
Donna Tartt

Character, to me, is the life blood of fiction.
Donna Tartt

There's an expectation these days that novels — like any other consumer product — should be made on a production line, with one dropping from the conveyor belt every couple of years.
Donna Tartt

A book is the writer's secret life, the dark
twin of a man; you can't reconcile them.
William Faulkner, *Mosquitos*

I believe that if art served any purpose at all, it would
at least keep the artists themselves occupied.
William Faulkner, *Mosquitos*

I write when the spirit moves me, and the spirit moves me every day.
William Faulkner

I was too busy and too mad all the time I was in California to write you.
William Faulkner, letter to Ben Wasson

Memory believes before knowing remembers.
William Faulkner, *Light in August*

I am telling the same story over and over,
which is myself and the world.
William Faulkner

Be born and raised in Mississippi — there's something
in the water there that makes outstanding writers.
Jo McDougall, Arkansas poet's advice to those who aspire to be writers

There's a black sheep in everybody's family, and
Billy's ours. He's not worth a cent.
Judge John Falkner, on William Faulkner
What you choose to not put in a story is as important as what you use.
Kevin Sessums

I found out that not only each book had to have a design, but the whole output or sum of an artist's work had to have design.

William Faulkner

Reading (Faulkner) was stream-of-unconsciousness; a tale of sound and fury, told by an idiot, signifying who-the-hell knows.

Jim Dees, *The Statue & the Fury*

If you want to sell books, you have to write about the interesting lawyers — the guys who steal all the money and take off.

John Grisham

If you can go see the movie or buy the book, buy the book.

John Grisham

Author Bio

David Crews serves as clerk of court for the U.S. District Court in the Northern District of Mississippi. He is a former United States Marshal who spent 12 years with the U.S. Justice Department in a variety of law enforcement and anti-terrorism roles.

Early in his career, David worked for Governor William Winter, serving on the Governor's senior staff. In that position, he helped secure passage of pioneering legislation that brought a statewide system of kindergartens, reading aides, compulsory school attendance, and other reforms to Mississippi. He was one of a handful of Winter staffers known as the "Boys of Spring."

In the 1980s, he served as executive director of CREATE, the state's largest community foundation.

In 2014, David produced a feature-length documentary film, *The Toughest Job*, that won a regional Emmy for Best Historical Documentary.

Among other initiatives he helped raise $2 million to construct the Mississippi Children's Cancer Clinic at the University Medical Center.

In his twenties, David hiked the entire 450 miles of the Natchez Trace from Natchez to Nashville. He is thought to be the first person to hike that ancient trail since the 1800s. His trek was chronicled in a National Geographic book on America's scenic trails.

David graduated magna cum laude and Phi Beta Kappa from the University of the South in Sewanee, Tennessee, where he worked on the Sewanee Fire Department. He is a mountain climber and marathoner who has climbed some of the world's highest peaks and competed in the Hawaiian Ironman Triathlon.

David and his wife, Claire, have twins affectionately known as the doublets. They live on a farm outside Oxford with five ferocious but lovable dogs.

Index

A

B

H

I

J

K

L

M

N

O

P

Q

R

S

T

U

ADDENDUM
2022

ATTITUDE

These folks don't scare me.
I've been booed by a whole stadium full of people.
Robert Khayat

There is only all or nothing. There is no in between.
Michael Farris Smith, *The Fighter*

How you deal with good is just as important as how you deal with bad.
Brett Favre

Challenge yourself, it's the only path that leads to growth.
Morgan Freeman

The trick to any profession is to make it look easy.
Morgan Freeman

The best way to guarantee a loss is to quit.
Morgan Freeman

You have to play it like you mean it.
Eudora Welty, *The Wells* **(Unpublished short story)**

BEAUTY

One single beautiful image is practically inexhaustible.
Walter Anderson

BLUES

I have the blues before sunrise, tears standing in my eyes.
John Lee Hooker

People like us — planters and landowners — often caused the pain these musicians turned into beauty.
Wright Thompson on Blues musicians

Blues fallin' down like hail... there's a hell hound on my trail.
Robert Johnson

CIVIL RIGHTS

The white people concluded it was unnecessary to wait the result
of the investigation – that it was preferable to hang the accused
first and try him afterward.
Ida B. Wells

A moral reckoning is upon us, and we have to decide, once and for all,
whether or not we will truly be a multiracial democracy.
Eddie Glaude, Jr., Begin Again

CULTURE

Art is a mysterious business.
Walter Anderson

DEATH

A knowledge of how to live was a knowledge of how to die.
Richard Wright, *Native Son*

DRINKING

Thirty days seem like years in a Jailhouse with no booze.
Charlie Patton, *High Sheriff Blues*

Don't ever knock a bottle out of my hand.
Robert Johnson

Drinking alcohol is the worst thing to do in cold weather.
Hot soup is the best.
Morgan Freeman

FOOTBALL

I think my stubbornness, hardheadedness, and stupidity is
what has allowed me to play for 20 years.
Brett Favre

You're only as good as your next pass.
Brett Favre

HISTORY

For any community, there are often vast differences between
public history and public relations.
Stephen Monroe, *Heritage & Hate*

What is the cost of knowing our past? And what is the cost of not?
Wright Thompson, *The Cost of These Dreams*

Our America is frightened of fact, of history, of process, of necessity. It
hugs the easy way of damning those it cannot understand.
Richard Wright

People always want to be on the right side of history; It is a lot easier to
say 'what an atrocity that was' than it is to say 'what an atrocity this is.
Natasha Trethewey

I don't want Black History Month. Black history is American history.
Morgan Freeman

HUMAN NATURE

If there is one thing the lost are able to recognize it is the others
who are just as lost and wandering.
Michael Farris Smith, *Nick*

Some people are all right. Some people ain't.
Michael Farris Smith, *Rivers*

How unbecoming for an elder man to drink beer with his young son in a darkened place before noon. What a bad example for the constituency of the good to profess so little respect for the office of fatherhood.

John Crews, *Unbecoming*

Families stay together because of active decisions, because of patterns that turn into rituals, and they are torn apart most often not by anger or feuds but by careless inertia.

Wright Thompson, *Pappyland*

There was a time when all I cared about was the next game, the next party, the next tee time.

Brett Favre

We should all remember that we are at once miracles and disasters.

Eddie Glaude, Jr., *Begin Again*

Rules imposed by government are important but often of limited value. What we really need are rules in our hearts.

Suzette Shelmire

HUMAN SPIRIT

We all get what we want. Each painter who paints a picture puts into it exactly what he wants. If he fails it is because he didn't want enough.

Walter Anderson

Never let pride be your guiding principle.
Let your accomplishments speak for you.

Morgan Freeman

Fatigue, discomfort, discouragement are merely symptoms of effort.

Morgan Freeman

You measure yourself by the people who measure themselves by you.

Morgan Freeman

HUMOR

You might be a redneck if your front porch collapses
and four dogs git killed.
Jerry Clower

You know a man is a redneck if there's two boys
in the same family named Jr.
Jerry Clower

That's absurd. That's like saying I should be
in an ad for Weight Watchers.
Haley Barbour

JUSTICE

One had better die fighting against injustice
than to die like a dog in a trap.
Ida B. Wells

There must always be a remedy for wrong and injustice
if we only know how to find it.
Ida B. Wells

LIES

If I die with a lie on my soul, I shall be tortured forever.
Ida B. Wells

Whites will tell you, 'we don't see race.' Biggest lie ever told.
Bennie Thompson

…we are all lying, every single one of us, one way or another.
David Magee, *Dear William*

The lie is the lifeblood of Trumpism.
Eddie Glaude, Jr., *Begin Again*

If a man confessed anything on his death bed, it was the truth;
for no man could stare death in the face and lie.
Richard Wright

LIFE

Life is good to me. How do you be good to life? You live it.
Morgan Freeman

Snatching the eternal out of the desperately fleeting
is the great magic trick of human existence.
Tennessee Williams

What do we value? Lies or facts. Posturing or morality.
Ace Atkins, *The Shameless*

We build a life to share, so that some idea of us can live
in our children and grandchildren, so that we might live forever
and they might never be alone.
Wright Thompson, *Pappyland*

That which does not kill us hurts like hell.
Bill Thames (with apologies to Friedrich Nietzsche)

I found the simple life weren't so simple.
Robert Johnson, *Runnin' With The Devil*

Their constant outward-looking, their mania for radios, cars, and a
thousand other trinkets made them dream and fix their eyes upon the
trash of life, made it impossible for them… to speak of what was in their
or others' hearts.
Richard Wright, *Black Boy*

Goddamnit, look! We live here and they live there. We black and they
white. They got things and we ain't. They do things and we can't.
It's just like livin' in jail.
Richard Wright, *Native Son*

Life does not spare us.
Jesmyn Ward, *Salvage the Bones*

Your only as good as your last pass.

Brett Favre

Every day is not perfect.

Brett Favre

LOVE

Love of sports will always break your heart, but in doing so,
it reminds us we have one.

Stuart Stevens, *The Last Season*

I'm in the mood baby, I'm in the mood for love.

John Lee Hooker

The heart is the thing that counts.

Walter Anderson

Love grows from stable relationships, shared experiences,
loyalty, devotion, trust.

Richard Wright

What is love/ One name for it is knowledge.

Natasha Trethewey, *Thrall*

MEN

A man often spends his entire adult life trying to be exactly
like his father or nothing like him.

Wright Thompson, *Pappyland*

A man's pursuit of knowledge is greater than his shortcomings.

Natasha Trethewey, *Thrall*

Man is a wasteful fool.

Walter Anderson

To realize the beauty of man, we must realize his relation to nature.

Walter Anderson

The world of man is far away and so is man. How pleasant without him.
Walter Anderson

Man exists and he is almost as wonderful as the thing he sees.
Walter Anderson

A man who runs in one direction may be caught by anyone, but a man that runs in three directions can't be caught.
Walter Anderson

MONEY

The appeal to the white man's pocket has ever been more effectual than all the appeals ever made to his conscience.
Ida B. Wells

The sincerest form of flattery in show business is a check that doesn't bounce.
David Sheffield

Wealth is not in making money, but in making the man while he is making money.
Roger Wicker

Money is becoming one of the most corrosive elements of politics.
Trent Lott

MISSISSIPPI

To find a good Mississippi story you have to explore the silences – the things people don't talk about.
Ralph Eubanks

In Mississippi confederate rhetoric remains active, loud, and influential.
Stephen Monroe, *Heritage & Hate*

Today's Mississippi is not the Mississippi of the movies. Thank God. It's far more complicated and beautiful. There is more hope.
Stephen Monroe, *Heritage & Hate*

MULES

A real black woman will make a mule kick his stable down.
Son House, *My Black Mama*

NATURE

There's too much blank sky where a tree once stood.
Jesmyn Ward, *Sing, Unburied, Sing*

Longing for a vanished agrarian past dominates much
of the American story.
Wright Thompson, *Pappyland*

There is a sensation of music – as if the leaves were notes – and an
accompaniment of sound changes with the color of the leaves.
Walter Anderson

If I destroy nature, and if nature is my source, I destroy myself.
Walter Anderson

NEWS MEDIA

The people must know before they can act, and there is
no educator to compare with the press.
Ida B. Wells

POLITICS

In politics purity is the enemy of victory.
Haley Barbour

Talk Radio is running America. We have to deal with that problem.
Trent Lott

If the Republican Party had been in charge in 1776,
we'd all still be celebrating the queen's birthday.
Stuart Stevens, *It Was All a Lie*

One of the hallmarks of the Trump era is the alacrity
with which intelligent people embrace stupidity.
Stuart Stevens, *It Was All a Lie*

I would do away with partisan political parties and would pit the
'aginner' party against the 'do gooder' party. The 'aginners' would
defend our failed status quo and the 'do betters' would propose ideas to
improve our quality of life.
Dick Molpus

Donald Trump's presidency unleashed forces howling beneath
our politics since the tumult of the 1960's.
Eddie Glaude, Jr., *Begin Again*

Corporations consolidated their hold on government.... Ideas of the
public good were reduced to an unrelenting pursuit of self-interest.
Eddie Glaude, Jr., *Begin Again*

Those whirlpools of politics that had the power to claim
the whole of men's souls.
Richard Wright, *Black Boy*

RELIGION

He could never get used to sitting next to men who sang hymns of love
and forgiveness knowing what they'd done. Yes, I raped. Yes, I took
another life. Yes, I stole. Yes, I raised a fist to my fellow man. But now I
have found the love of God. Now I see the light. Now I am found and on
and on to a smattering of amens and hallelujahs and praise the Lords
until Russell couldn't take it anymore and so he gave up. He didn't believe it worked that way and if it did then something didn't seem right.
Michael Farris Smith, *Desperation Road*

I'm going to be a Baptist Preacher/ And I sure won't have to work.
Son House, *Preachin' the Blues*

My God is a spiral without beginning or end.
Walter Anderson

The white folks like for us to be religious, then they
can do what they want with us.
Richard Wright, *Native Son*

On his death bed a man claimed he saw the bright lights of
heaven. Another man in the hospital room whispered, "He saw a
light alright. But trust me, it wasn't the bright lights of heaven he saw.
It was the burning fires of hell.'
Anonymous comment at Baptist Hospital

The highest power is the human mind. That's where God came
from and my belief in God is my belief in myself.
Morgan Freeman

SEX

The best thing about shaking from Parkinson's disease
is that you never know when sex is over.
Soggy Sweat

THE SOUTH

I was leaving the South to fling myself into the unknown…
respond to the warmth of other suns and perhaps to bloom.
Richard Wright

My mother's people were of the Deep South – emotional, changeable,
touched with charisma, and given to histrionic flourishes. They were
courageous under tension and unexpectedly tough beneath their wild
eccentricities, for they had an unusually close working agreement with
God. They also had an unusually high quota of bullshit.
Willie Morris

I can think of no one more qualified to write about
the modern South than Curtis Wilkie.
Willie Morris

TROUBLE

I was raised in the country been working in the town/
I've been in trouble since I set my suitcase down.
Bob Dylan, *Mississippi*

The night was beyond his control.
David Magee, *Dear William*

The idea of America is in deep trouble.
Eddie Glaude, Jr., *Begin Again*

The future will damn sure be hard.
Eddie Glaude, Jr., *Begin Again*

TRUTH

The way to right wrongs is to turn the light of truth upon them.
Ida B. Wells

Republicans are linked to a vast life-support system of lies,
terrified that the truth will unplug the machine.
Stuart Stevens, *It Was All a Lie*

Eyes reveal the truth, and eyes cannot hide lies and pain.
David Magee, *Dear William*

The pretending and covering up became more real than the truth.
David Magee, *Dear William*

I did not know if the story was factually true or not,
but it was emotionally true.
Richard Wright, *Black Boy*

VIOLENCE

A Winchester rifle should have a place of honor in every black home, and
it should be used for that protection which the law refuses to give.
Ida B. Wells

The first thing you want to do after being shot is
make sure you are not shot again.
Ace Atkins

VIRTUE

Virtue knows no color line.
Ida B. Wells

WRITING

Every beginning writer has a certain quota of mediocrity to fill.
David Sheffield, *The Heartbreak Henry*

I think writing has a cleansing effect and although it is easy enough to
keep the body clean, the mind seems to grow clogged.
Walter Anderson

It's easy to tell a story, but it's difficult to tell a good story.
David Magee, *Dear William*

Whenever my environment failed to support me, I clutched at books.
Richard Wright

All literature is protest.
Richard Wright

Literature is a struggle over the nature of reality.
Richard Wright, *Native Son*

I believe there is power in words, power in asserting our existence, our experience, our lives, through words.

Jesmyn Ward, *The Fire This Time*

It took me years to understand that words are often as important as experience, because words make experience last.

Willie Morris, *North Toward Home*

It's living that makes me want to write, not reading – although it's reading that makes me love writing.

Eudora Welty

If it happened – tell it.

Eudora Welty, *The Wells*